Sociology as a Population Science

John Goldthorpe is one of Britain's most eminent sociologists and a strong advocate of quantitative sociology. In this concise and accessible book, he provides a new rationale for recent developments in sociology which focus on establishing and explaining probabilistic regularities in human populations. Through these developments, Goldthorpe shows how sociology has become more securely placed within the 'probabilistic revolution' that has occurred over the last century in the natural and social sciences alike. The central arguments of the book are illustrated with examples from different areas of sociology, ranging from social stratification and the sociology of the family to the sociology of revolutions. He concludes by considering the implications of these arguments for the proper boundaries of sociology, for its relations with other disciplines, and for its public role.

JOHN H. GOLDTHORPE is Emeritus Fellow of Nuffield College, University of Oxford.

Sociology as a Population Science

JOHN H. GOLDTHORPE

Nuffield College, Oxford

CAMBRIDGE
UNIVERSITY PRESS

CAMBRIDGE
UNIVERSITY PRESS

University Printing House, Cambridge CB2 8BS, United Kingdom

Cambridge University Press is part of the University of Cambridge.

It furthers the University's mission by disseminating knowledge in the pursuit of
education, learning and research at the highest international levels of excellence.

www.cambridge.org
Information on this title: www.cambridge.org/9781107567313

© John H. Goldthorpe 2016

First published 2016

Printed in the United States of America by Sheridan Books, Inc.

A catalogue record for this publication is available from the British Library

ISBN 978-1-107-12783-8 Hardback
ISBN 978-1-107-56731-3 Paperback

For Raffi – who came too late for the last one.

Contents

Acknowledgements

This book began life as a draft journal article, which, like Topsy, 'just grow'd'. It eventually attained a length far beyond what any journal would find acceptable, and so I faced a decision on whether to cut back the draft severely or to extend it further with a book in mind. Another option that sometimes seemed, in dark moments, attractive was simply to put what I had written into a drawer and forget about it. That the present work did eventually emerge is due in large part to the support I received from colleagues, three of whom have to be given particular mention.

At a critical moment, Francesco Billari read my initial draft, made a series of very helpful comments and came out strongly in favour of my developing it into a book. He also, although unknowingly, provided me with further encouragement to do so by creating a context in which this appeared a worthwhile endeavour: that is, through his revitalisation of sociology in Oxford since his arrival in 2012.

Over a much longer period, I have benefited greatly from the knowledge and wise counsel of David Cox. He too read my initial draft, and also the first version of the present text, and made many valuable suggestions, especially, although not only, in regard to statistical issues. Such insight into these issues as I possess I have very largely gained through conversations with David – although, I hasten to add, he is in no way responsible for any deficiencies in my understanding that remain and that may well become apparent in the pages that follow. More indirectly, but no less importantly, David has been a source of further support from the time he became Warden of Nuffield College in 1988, in virtue of the model he provides of the scientific attitude and indeed of the scientific life.

Throughout the years in which this book has been in gestation, I have collaborated with Erzsébet Bukodi in a series of research projects, and our many discussions – often of a 'lively' nature – on the direction and strategy of our research and on the interpretation of our findings have influenced the content of the book in many ways. Still more valuable, though, has been the unfailing encouragement and help that Erzsébet has given me in persisting with the task in hand and in urging on me a spirit of optimism when this was most needed. It is indeed difficult for me to envisage how the book could ever have been written if she had not been there.

I am indebted to several other colleagues who read and commented on the first version of the book in whole or in part. These include – with remorseful apologies to anyone I may have overlooked – Michael Biggs, Ferdinand Eibl, Robert Erikson, Duncan Gallie, Michelle Jackson and Jouni Kuha. Others who have given me helpful advice and information are Tak Wing Chan, John Darwin, Nan Dirk De Graaf, Geoff Evans, David Hand, Colin Mills, Christiaan Monden, Reinhard Pollak, David Rose, Antonio Schizzerotto, Jan Vandenbroucke and Yu Xie.

I am grateful to the Warden and Fellows of Nuffield for the generosity they show towards emeriti in providing them with a full range of facilities in the College, not least of which are the admirable services of the library staff and of secretarial and IT support personnel.

Finally, I should acknowledge the continuing tolerance of my wife and family of my non-retirement from academic work and of the absences, mental if not corporeal, that this often entails.

Introduction

This book follows on from, and at various points exploits, my earlier work *On Sociology* (2nd edn 2007). It has, however, a significantly different character. *On Sociology* was a collection of rather diverse essays that were brought together under the headings of 'Critique and Program' (volume 1) and 'Illustration and Retrospect' (volume 2). These essays were mainly written around the turn of the century – a time of intense debate over how sociology as an academic and intellectual enterprise should be viewed and of great uncertainty over the future course of its development. During more recent years I have become aware of a significantly changing situation. Some at least of the kinds of sociology that I earlier criticised – for example, 'grand' historical sociology and 'post-modernist' ethnography – would appear to have fallen into decline; and, of greater consequence, the version of sociology that I argued for programmatically and sought to illustrate has, at least in certain respects, flourished to a degree that I find surprising – although, of course, pleasantly so. I would naturally like to see evidence here of the influence of *On Sociology*; but, as a good Popperian, I have to accord crucial importance to the 'logic of the situation'. Research designed to address well-defined sociological problems and based on the quantitative analysis of extensive and high-quality data-sets – even if not backed by theoretical advance to the extent I might wish – has been increasingly recognised as having premium payoffs, in both its 'pure' and 'applied' aspects, and has in turn become increasingly attractive to working sociologists and to funding agencies alike.[1]

---

[1] The main exception to this general statement unfortunately arises with my own country, Great Britain, where, especially within university departments as distinct

Consequently, there now appears to be less need than previously for critical or programmatic interventions, and I would, in turn, wish to emphasise the following point regarding the present work. In seeking to make out the case for an understanding of sociology as a population science, my main concern is not to propose to sociologists how they should conceive of and practise their subject. It is rather to suggest a way in which a fuller and more explicit rationale than has hitherto been available might be provided *for what a large and steadily growing number of sociologists in fact already do* – although, perhaps, without a great deal of reflection on the matter. If asked what purpose the elaboration of such a rationale might serve, my response would be twofold. First, I believe that some greater awareness on the part of the sociologists in question of what it is that they are about should enable them to proceed more systematically and effectively in their everyday work. And second, I believe that, as well as helping to create such awareness, an understanding of sociology as a population science affords the best basis on which these sociologists can articulate and pursue a goal in which, I believe, they would largely share: that is, the goal of developing sociology as a science in a sense that allows for a meaningful degree of continuity with the natural sciences while still preserving sociology's proper distinctiveness.

It may well be that some of the sociologists I have here in mind will not be ready to accept my interpretation of the sociology in which they engage as constituting, or even as moving in the direction of, a

from – often interdisciplinary – research centres, a strong hostility to quantitative sociology persists. Interestingly, my earlier book, while widely reviewed elsewhere, whether in its original form or in later Italian, Polish and Spanish versions, was not reviewed in *Sociology*, the official journal of the British Sociological Association, nor in the *Sociological Review*. But even perhaps in Britain, 'the times they are a-changin'. The Q-Step programme, launched in 2013, with a budget of £19.5 million, aims to substantially extend and revitalise the quantitative training of social science undergraduates. It will, I hope, achieve its goals in sociology, despite efforts that are, apparently, in train to subvert it. A number of remarkably ill-informed claims have of late been made to the effect that quantitative methods of a kind labelled as 'conventional' are now largely outmoded and irrelevant and should be replaced by others (e.g. Byrne, 2012; Castellani, 2014). Some of the alternative methods proposed are critically considered in the course of the chapters that follow.

population science, nor again my view that this represents the most promising way ahead for a scientific sociology. Responses to my book made on these lines I would regard as very welcome ones – provided that they are accompanied by alternative interpretations of how sociology is in fact developing as a science and by some indications of how this development might best be furthered. Discussion of the issues that are likely to arise in this connection could be of particular value at the present time.

I do, of course, also recognise that there are many other sociologists who would disagree with me in a more fundamental way: that is, in doubting that sociology can claim scientific status and indeed in believing that it is not even desirable that it should try to do so. These sociologists I would regard as selling sociology short – as standing in the way of it realising its full potential – and I can have little common ground with them. Moreover, I can now see little point in engaging further in the already protracted debates that have taken place on this matter: the future will decide.

In writing this book, I have aimed at clarity and brevity. In the interests of clarity, the book is structured around nine propositions. One of these propositions stands at the head of each of the central chapters, and the chapter itself is then given over to elaborating and supporting the proposition. Readers who would like to have an initial overview of the argument of the book can simply read through the propositions. In advancing the case for sociology as a population science, I have found it necessary to cover a rather wide terrain and to refer to literature from a range of different fields apart from that of sociology itself. However, in the interests of brevity I have in general indicated only the essentials of the way in which I would see the work on which I draw as being relevant to the positions I take up, and I have then left it to readers to use the citations given in order to check, if they so wish, that my use of these sources is appropriate. It may be noted that, for a short book, there is a rather long set of references.

In one respect, I have given some weight to clarity as against brevity. Insofar as the arguments I advance are of a general and abstract character, I have tried to bring out more clearly the main points that they seek to make by providing particular and concrete illustrations. In the case of specifically sociological arguments, these illustrations may perhaps be thought to be too often taken from my own fields of research interest, in particular social stratification and mobility. But, to the extent that my knowledge has allowed, I have entered into other fields as well.

The book is aimed primarily at professional sociologists and at more advanced students. I have therefore assumed a certain amount of background knowledge, including some basic technical knowledge in relation to methods of data collection and analysis. However, I have kept the text itself as non-technical as possible: there are no formulae or equations. At the same time, though, I have found expository advantage, in particular in the chapters dealing with issues of data collection and analysis, in taking a historical approach. Robert Merton once complained (1957: 4) that in discussion of sociological theory, too much attention was given to history at the expense of what he called 'systematics'. But as regards the discussion of research methods in sociology, one could almost make the opposite complaint. That is to say, too little attention is given to why methods presently in use are as they are. Why did these methods emerge? What preceded them? What were the problems for which they provided better solutions, and how? Addressing such questions seems to me to be often highly illuminating.

In completion of this Introduction, there are two further observations of a more personal kind that I might make. The first refers back to my earlier remark that over recent years I have become aware of a significant change in sociology in the research styles that are assuming prominence – a change that I find highly congenial and that led me to believe that there might be some point in a book of the kind I have now written. I would like here further to say that the main context within which this change was borne in on me was that provided by the European sociological research community: in particular, by conferences and workshops organised by the

European Consortium for Sociological Research and also under the auspices of two EU-funded 'Networks of Excellence' in sociology – CHANGEQUAL and its successor, EQUALSOC.[2]

With American readers chiefly in mind, I might add here that there has been some tendency within American sociology to see the most distinctive European contributions to the subject as being made at rather rarefied levels of theory or at the intersection of methodological and philosophical issues (with an attendant exaggeration of the importance of some, chiefly French and German, authors). While this view was always questionable, it is by now quite clearly out of date. Over the last twenty years or so there has been a rather remarkable expansion of sociological research, of a largely quantitative character, in almost all of the major European countries – research that is of a technical standard quite comparable to that of American work and that is often of at least potentially greater theoretical interest, in having a comparative cross-national or cross-regional basis.[3] I frequently draw on this body of research for my illustrative purposes. In addition, it could be noted that it is European sociologists who have been prominent in developing the 'mechanism-based' approach to causal explanation that, as discussed especially in Chapter 9, I would regard as most appropriate to sociology understood as a population science.

[2] The partner institutions in the CHANGEQUAL network were the Economic and Social Research Institute, Dublin; the Centre National de la Recherche Scientifique EHSS LASMAS, Paris; the Swedish Institute for Social Research, University of Stockholm; the Zentrum für Europäische Sozialforschung, University of Mannheim; and my own institution, Nuffield College, Oxford. In the EQUALSOC network, the CNRS institution became GENES/GRECSTA and eight further institutions were added: the Institute for Advanced Labour Studies, University of Amsterdam; the Centre for Social Policy, Antwerp; the Universita Degli Studi di Milano Bicocca; the Department of Political and Social Science, University of Pompeu Fabra, Barcelona; the Department of Sociology and Social Policy, University of Tartu; the Department of Social Sciences, University of Turin; the Department of Sociology and Social Research, University of Trento; and the Wissenschaftzentrum für Sozialforschung, Berlin.

[3] The British exception has again to be noted. At the conferences and workshops referred to in the text, the virtual absence of young British researchers has been sadly apparent.

My second, more personal observation is the following. I have written this book somewhere towards the end of a rather long life in academia (a circumstance in itself favouring brevity), and my views have obviously been in various respects influenced by my own experiences over the years in question. Indeed, in some instances I have made this quite explicit, and especially where I have to acknowledge the influence of a teacher or a colleague. I would like to think that in this way also the book benefits from a historical perspective – and one that is, I would suggest, much needed in order to offset sociology's rather manifest lack of collective memory, leading to an unfortunate neglect of the deeper origins of current problems and often in turn to the rediscovery of wheels. But I realise that I might equally well be regarded as harking back unduly to issues that have been long forgotten, and with good reason.[4] At all events, examples of what might be regarded as my anecdotage have been largely confined to the notes.

---

[4] A reviewer of a paper that a similarly aged colleague and I recently submitted to a leading sociological journal objected to the fact that articles were cited that were published before he or she was born. Clearly, nothing of importance could have happened before that date.

I Sociology as a population science: the central idea

Sociology should be understood as a population science in the sense of Neyman (1975).

On the occasion of the 500th anniversary of the birth of Nicholas Copernicus (1473–1543), the US National Academy of Sciences sponsored a collection of essays on 'quasi-Copernican' scientific revolutions. The volume was edited by the Polish-born statistician Jerzy Neyman, who supplied brief introductions to its several sections. In one such introduction, to a series of essays on 'The Study of Chance Mechanisms – A Quasi-Copernican Revolution in Science and Mathematics', Neyman (1975: 417) made the following observation:

> Beginning with the nineteenth century, and increasing in the twentieth, science brought about 'pluralistic' subjects of study, categories of entities satisfying certain definitions but varying in their individual properties. Technically, such categories are called 'populations'.

Neyman emphasised that populations in this technical sense could, substantively, be of quite different kinds. They could be human or other animal populations, but also populations of, say, molecules or galaxies. The common feature of such populations was that, while their individual elements were subject to considerable variability and might appear, at least in some respects, indeterminate in their states and behaviour, they could nonetheless *exhibit aggregate-level regularities of a probabilistic kind.*[1]

---

[1] I was first directed to Neyman's remarks by a reference to them in Duncan (1984: 96). As will become readily apparent, Dudley Duncan is an author to whom I am

The aims of a science dealing with such pluralistic subjects of study – or, that is, of what could be called a 'population science' – were then twofold. The initial aim was to investigate, and to establish, the probabilistic regularities that characterise a particular population, or its appropriately defined subpopulations. In this regard, Neyman saw the use of statistical methods of both data collection and analysis as being essential. And indeed, fifty years previously, R. A. Fisher (1925: 2) had already *defined* statistics as 'the study of populations, or aggregates of individuals', and had represented statistics as foundational for all sciences that were primarily concerned with the properties of aggregates rather than of their individual members. It may moreover be noted, in view of what is to follow, that Fisher then added the remark that 'Statistical methods are essential to social studies, and it is principally by the aid of such methods that these studies may be raised to the rank of science.'[2]

However, Neyman also made it clear that once population regularities had been empirically established, the further aim of a population science had to be that of determining the processes or 'mechanisms' which *in their operation at the individual level* actually produced these regularities. And since the regularities – the explananda of a population science – were probabilistic, the mechanisms that would need to be envisaged would be ones that, rather than being entirely grounded in deterministic laws, *incorporated chance*. A new form of scientific explanation was implied.

Neyman's claim that from the nineteenth into the twentieth century the increasing study of 'pluralistic' entities on a statistical

indebted in many other respects. He must be regarded as one of the great pioneers in conceptualising and practising sociology as a population science. Another who contributed significantly, although in a less explicit way, was my former teacher at the London School of Economics, David Glass – now shamefully disremembered in British sociology – under the influence of his own teacher, the extraordinary polymath Lancelot Hogben (see Hogben, 1938).

2 Neyman and Fisher were of course the leading antagonists in what has been described as 'the widest cleft in statistics' over issues of hypothesis-testing. But, as Louçã (2008: 4) has observed, in their vision of statistics as the language for a new form of science, they were in fact 'quite close'.

basis marked a scientific revolution has been amply justified by later work in the history of science. What has in fact become known as the 'probabilistic revolution' (Krüger, Daston and Heidelberger, 1987; Krüger, Gigerenzer and Morgan, 1987) is now widely recognised as one of the most – if not the most – momentous intellectual developments of the period in question. 'In 1800', to quote Hacking (1987: 52), 'we are in the deterministic world so aptly characterised by Laplace. By 1936 we are firmly in a world that is ultimately indeterminate . . . Chance, which, for Hume, was "nothing real" was, for von Neumann, perhaps the only reality.'[3] However, as Hacking goes on to stress (see also Hacking, 1990), it is important to see that complementary to 'the erosion of determinism' was 'the taming of chance': that is, the process of making chance and its consequences intelligible and manageable on the twin bases of assemblages of numerical data and the application of probability theory.

In the early stages of the probabilistic revolution, the social sciences did in fact play a leading part. In particular, Quetelet's application (1835/1842, 1846, 1869) of the Gaussian 'error curve' – or the normal distribution – to the display of regularities in the 'moral statistics' of marriage, illegitimacy, suicide and crime represented a pioneering attempt to show how a higher-level probabilistic order could emerge from out of individual actions that were generally supposed to be non-deterministic in character, or, that is, to express individual will and choice (Porter, 1986: chs 2, 6 esp.). And the notable development then was that the influence of Quetelet's work extended from the social into the natural sciences – somewhat ironically, given his great ambition to create a 'social physics'. As Krüger (1987: 80) has observed, at this point 'the familiar hierarchy of the disciplines' was inverted.

---

[3] Hacking is here referring to von Neumann's mathematical formulation of quantum theory. This aimed to preclude the possibility of 'hidden variables' that, if identified, would allow for phenomena that otherwise appeared probabilistic to be understood as deterministic – so that particles possessed a definite position and velocity at all times. For an accessible account, see Kumar (2008: ch. 14).

Most notably, Quetelet's use of the error curve provided a model for James Clerk Maxwell in his development of the kinetic theory of gases (Gillispie, 1963; Porter, 1982). Within a gas, the lower-level processes of colliding molecules were, in principle, subject to deterministic Newtonian laws; but the vast numbers of molecules involved meant that, in practice, a probabilistic treatment – 'statistical physics' – was required. In work carried out in the later 1860s, Maxwell took a version of the error curve to represent the *distribution* of molecular velocities within an ideal gas, so that, while nothing could be said about individual molecules, it became possible to calculate the *proportion* of molecules with velocities within a given range at any given temperature. Maxwell was generous in his acknowledgement of his borrowing in this regard from Quetelet and his followers. In speaking to the British Association for the Advancement of Science, he referred to physicists adopting a method of analysis new to them but which 'has long been in use in the section of Statistics' (cited in Gigerenzer et al., 1989: 62; see also Mahon, 2003: ch. 6).[4]

Subsequently, Fisher (1922), in seeking to integrate Mendelism into Darwin's evolutionary theory, adopted a model closely analogous to that which Maxwell had taken over from Quetelet, with biological populations corresponding to the populations of molecules. Under this model, natural selection could be seen as operating amid a multiplicity of random causes – any of which might have a predominant influence at the level of a particular individual – while, however, the probabilistic processes of natural selection remained the key determinants of the evolution of the population as a whole (Morrison, 2002).

In association with such developments, evolutionary biology, as Ernst Mayr (2001; see also 1982: ch. 2) has described, became the field in which the most explicit development of 'population thinking' occurred. In a scientific world dominated by physics and chemistry, what Mayr characterises as 'typological thinking' had prevailed,

---

[4] Ludwig Boltzmann, another pioneer of statistical physics, was also influenced by the work of Quetelet and his followers and expositors (Porter, 1986: 125–8).

centred on the properties of – and the deterministic laws applying to – entities of a supposedly homogenous rather than a 'pluralistic' kind, such as nuclear particles or chemical elements. But in evolutionary biology, increasing recognition came to be given to *the variation existing within* the entities under study – that is, to variation among the individuals making up a population – while at the same time interest focused on the probabilistic regularities that were still discernible amid this variation and on the processes, or mechanisms, through which these regularities were created.[5]

In contrast, in the social sciences, despite their influential role in the origins of the probabilistic revolution, there was a failure to exploit the possibilities that it opened up in both research and theory. Sociology at least (see Goldthorpe, 2007: vol. 2, chs 8 and 9) can still be regarded as not having a fully resolved relationship with this revolution and with the new ways of scientific thinking that it prompted.[6] Few sociologists today would believe that they should aim at formulating deterministic laws in the manner attempted by Comte, Spencer or Marx, intended to provide a comprehensive understanding of the structure, functioning and development of human societies. But for those who would still wish to maintain the idea of sociology as being, at least potentially, a science of some kind, the issue remains – and has been remarkably little addressed – of just what kind of science this might be. More specifically, if the search for deterministic laws in sociology is misconceived, then one may ask: to what objectives *is* sociological enquiry to be orientated and how is one to understand the rationale of the research activities that are carried out in their pursuit? As I indicated in the Introduction, the proposition that sociology should be understood as a population science is directed towards

---

[5] I am indebted to Yu Xie for drawing my attention to Mayr's remarkable work and to its relevance – as will later emerge – to current issues in sociology. See further Xie (2005).

[6] For interesting discussion of the – eventual – accommodation of economics to the probabilistic revolution, see the papers in Krüger, Gigerenzer and Morgan (1987: part III).

answering these questions, and at the same time towards situating sociology more securely within the probabilistic revolution.

What is implied, to put the matter at its broadest, is the following. The concern of sociology should be with populations or sub-populations of _Homo sapiens_ (or better, perhaps – see Chapter 2 – of _Homo sapiens sapiens_) in their location in place and time; and the goal of sociological enquiry should be an understanding, not of the states and behaviour of the particular individual members of such populations in all their variability, but rather of the regularities that are the properties of these populations themselves, even though they are emergent only from the behaviour or – more precisely, as will later be argued – from the _actions_ of their individual members.

To spell out more fully what is entailed by this primary proposition will be the task of the chapters that follow, each starting from its own subsidiary proposition. In conclusion of the present chapter, I add some further preliminary remarks concerning regularities in human populations and their determination and explanation. These may help to provide a context for the course of the subsequent argument and to signpost a number of major issues that will arise.

The regularities that can be identified in human populations, and more specifically in human social life, are diverse in their range and in their complexity. The regularities in 'moral statistics' to which Quetelet initially drew attention were relatively simple ones relating to the stability over time of rates of different kinds of individual actions and of their outcomes in national or regional populations. But Quetelet himself was forced eventually to recognise not only differences in such rates across these populations, but also significant differences _among their various subpopulations;_ that is, among different groupings of individuals as defined in terms of age, gender, ethnicity, occupation and so on. And in this latter regard, he was then led to move on from essentially bivariate analyses to what can be recognised as early attempts at the multivariate analysis of social regularities of the kind that would be standard in present-day research (see esp. Quetelet, 1835/1842: part 3 with reference to crime rates).

In sociology today, the complexity of the regularities on which attention centres is of course often much further increased. For example, the concern may be not only with regularities expressed in the stability of particular forms of individual action and their outcomes within populations or in prevailing differences among populations or their subpopulations, but also with *regularities in changes* in these respects over time – and where time may be treated with reference to historical periods, the succession of birth cohorts or the individual life-course. Or the focus may be on regularities that exist between patterns of individual action and the locations of individuals in micro-, meso- or macro-level social contexts, as represented, say, by primary groups, social networks, associations and organisations, or by institutional and other variable aspects of the wider social structure. Or again, interest may lie in seeking regularities entirely at the supra-individual level: for example, among the structural features of 'total' – national or state – societies.

However, there are two further aspects of regularities in human social life that, while associated with their degree of complexity, are, for present purposes, of more direct relevance: what could be called their *visibility* and their *transparency*.

Consider the following case. There is a marked regularity in the number of individuals who drive their cars past my house between the hours of 7 and 9 a.m. on weekdays, and a regular and substantial decline in the numbers who do so on Saturdays and Sundays. These regularities would be apparent in their general form to any casual observer, and a standard traffic count would serve to establish them with some precision. Further, one could in this case readily construct a simple – although, as will later be seen, what could still be regarded as a paradigmatic – account of how these regularities are brought about. That is, a causal narrative couched in terms of individuals' ends – on weekdays, typically those of getting to work or ferrying children to school – and of the courses of action through which they then seek to achieve these ends, given the various constraints and opportunities that define their conditions of action. In short, the regularities in question could be regarded as being both highly visible *and* transparent. It is relatively easy both to see them and to 'see through' them; that is, to see through them to the social processes through which they are generated and sustained.

In contrast, though, the regularities that would be more typically the concern of sociology as a population science would be ones that are neither so readily visible nor, moreover, so transparent even when made visible; and wide-ranging implications then follow for the practice of sociology if understood in the way in question. Thus, to fulfil the first aim of a population science – that is, to empirically establish population regularities – will generally require, in the case of human societies, considerable effort in data collection and analysis. What is entailed is the design and application of research procedures capable of revealing aggregate-level regularities that were previously perhaps only vaguely sensed, if not entirely unrecognised, within the societies in which they operate. For example, to revert to the regularities that preoccupied Quetelet and his followers in rates of marriage, illegitimacy, suicide and crime, the possibility of establishing these regularities on any reliable basis only arose once national governments began to develop the apparatus of what would now be called 'official statistics' including population censuses and various registration systems.[7]

And to move on to the present day, one could say that the main scientific achievement of sociological research, as based on population surveys of differing design and the analysis of the data

---

[7] It was lack of data of the kind in question that can be seen as chiefly impeding the efforts of the British 'political arithmeticians' of the seventeenth and earlier eighteenth centuries, such as John Graunt, William Petty, Gregory King and Edmond Halley. In their pioneering efforts in the field of demography, broadly conceived, they were forced to work – although typically with great resource and ingenuity – on a miscellany of limited and frequently faulty data drawn from land surveys, tax returns, parish records of births and deaths, bills of mortality and so on. I learnt much about these early population scientists from the research of David Glass (1973) and later from that of Richard Stone (1997), being privileged to be a member in the 1960s of the Department of Applied Economics at Cambridge, which was largely Stone's creation.

produced, has so far been its demonstrated capacity to reveal population regularities in the more complex forms earlier referred to – regularities which, without the methodology in question, powerfully reinforced by increasing computing power for the purposes of both the storage and the analysis of data, simply could not have been accessed.

To illustrate here from my own field of research, although many other examples could readily be provided, a large number of studies have by now been undertaken into patterns and trends of intergenerational social mobility – studies characterised by growing conceptual sophistication. In particular, a crucial distinction has been made between absolute and relative mobility rates, with the former referring to mobility as actually experienced by individuals and the latter comparing the chances of individuals of different social origins attaining different class destinations (see e.g. Grusky and Hauser, 1984; Goldthorpe, 1987; Erikson and Goldthorpe, 1992; Breen, 2004; Ishida, 2008). The extensive work of data collection and conceptually informed statistical modelling involved has brought out both population regularities in, and also historically specific features of, the societies studied *of a kind that could not otherwise have been observed* – and certainly not by the 'lay members' of these societies in the course of their everyday lives, despite the close connection in fact existing between the regularities and specificities in question and their own life-chances and life-choices.[8]

[8] It is of course the case that in social mobility research, as in other fields, some amount of disagreement can arise over exactly what are the regularities in evidence: for example, over whether a long-term tendency can be observed for relative mobility rates to become more equal rather than fluctuating in a trendless fashion. But while such disagreements may figure rather prominently in the current research literature, this should not be allowed to detract from the important degree of consensus that is often in other respects established: for example, in the case of mobility research, on the fact that change in absolute rates is overwhelmingly driven by structural effects rather than by change in relative rates, or on the fact that where changes in relative rates do occur, whether directional or otherwise, they are usually very slow, in that they tend to result from cohort replacement effects far more than from period effects.

However, to return to my earlier distinction, making population regularities visible does not imply making them transparent; that is, it does not imply fulfilling the second aim of a population science: that of determining the processes – or, one could say, the causal mechanisms – through which regularities established at the aggregate level are produced at the individual level. In the case of sociology, this must mean demonstrating how these regularities derive ultimately from individual action and interaction. And it has to be acknowledged that, if sociology can by now claim some genuine success as a population science so far as revealing population regularities is concerned, its achievements to date in making these regularities transparent – that is, in accounting for them in the way indicated – have been a good deal less impressive. Regularities that may have been described in a quite detailed form often remain more or less opaque. Social mobility research would, unfortunately, again provide a good illustration of the point.[9]

Distinguishing between the dual tasks of a population science aimed at making population regularities first visible and then transparent – the one essentially a task of description, the other of explanation – is of key importance. This will become increasingly apparent as the argument of subsequent chapters proceeds.

[9] My own initial attempt at remedying the situation can be found in Goldthorpe, 2007: vol. 2, ch. 7, on which I hope to build in the course of research in which I am currently engaged.

2 Individual variability in human social life

Sociology has to be understood as a population science, primarily on account of the degree of variability evident in human social life, at the level of sociocultural entities, but also, and crucially, at the individual level – this latter variability being inadequately treated within the 'holistic' paradigm of inquiry, for long prevalent in sociology but now increasingly called into question.

Human social life is characterised by very great variability across place and time. This can be understood as the consequence of the distinctive capacities of *Homo sapiens sapiens* – modern humans – for both culture and sociality. The following would, I believe, be generally accepted.

While a capacity for culture is not unique to human beings, it is in their case evolved to an exceptional degree, and primarily through their command of language, or, more generally, of symbolic communication (see e.g. Barrett, Dunbar and Lycett, 2002: chs 2, 3; Jablonka and Lamb, 2005: ch. 6). To a quite distinctive extent, humans are able to acquire, store and transmit what could be understood in a broad sense as *information.* That is, information about the world, material and social, in which they live, in the form of knowledge and its embodiment in skills and technologies; and also information about their own responses to this world, in the form of beliefs and values as expressed in myths, religions, rituals, customs and conventions, moral and legal codes, philosophies and ideologies, art forms and so on. But while the capacity for culture is generic, cultures themselves are particular. And across human populations, separated in place and time, the actual content of cultures and of their component subcultures has been shown to be extraordinarily diverse. Humans are far more variable than are members of all other species of animal: not, primarily, on account of greater variation in their genes or in the ecological conditions under which they live, but rather on account of the knowledge, beliefs and values that they acquire through processes of learning from others of their kind (Richerson and Boyd, 2005: 55–7; Plotkin, 2007).

Similarly, the human capacity for sociality, although not unique, is also exceptional in its degree, and in particular in its extension to non-kin. Underlying this capacity would appear to be humans' highly evolved 'theory of mind' (Baron-Cohen, 1991, 1995; Barrett, Dunbar and Lycett, 2002: ch. 11; Dunbar, 2004: ch. 3, 2014: ch. 2), which allows them not only to be aware of their own mental states but, further, to form ideas of the mental states of others, and up to several degrees ('I think that he feels that she wants . . . ' etc).[1] A theory of mind of this kind creates the possibility of intersubjectivity and thus of social action as distinct from, or at least as a special form of behaviour. It enables individuals to empathise with others and thus to anticipate, allow for and seek to influence what they might do, and in turn vastly increases the qualitative range of social relationships in which they can engage. It underlies, for example, all relationships involving trust or deceit, co-operation or defection, alliance or opposition. In conjunction with humans' capacity for culture, this 'ultra-sociality' can then be seen as the source of the enormous variability in the institutional and other social structural features that are documented across human societies, and that, once created, provide correspondingly diverse contexts within which patterns of social action are both motivated and constrained.

However, a crucial issue that then arises in sociological analysis is that of how this degree of variability in human social life is to be accommodated. Within what I shall refer to as the 'holistic paradigm',

---

[1] Much debate has gone on, and continues, over whether any other animals – for example, chimpanzees – can operate with a theory of mind of even one degree. In humans, a theory of mind is known to develop rapidly between the ages of three and five, but it is significant that this development appears to be impaired in autistic children (Baron-Cohen, 1995; Barrett, Dunbar and Lycett, 2002: 303–15).

variability is in effect treated as occurring essentially _among_ sociocultural entities at whatever more micro- or more macro-level they may be distinguished – whether, say, as tribes, local communities, ethnic groupings, social classes or even total, national or state, societies. Such entities are represented as more or less coherent and distinctive 'wholes' that in themselves are to be taken as the key units of analysis. Carrithers (1992: 17–19) has aptly referred in this regard to the 'sea-shell' view of cultures or societies: that is, as type-specimens that can be arrayed, as in a museum, for purposes of comparison and classification. And one can indeed readily recognise in the holistic paradigm the kind of typological thinking which, as noted in Chapter 1, Mayr would see as being prevalent in the natural and social sciences before the challenge of population thinking arose.

Within the holistic paradigm, much work has been of an expressly idiographic kind: that is, centred on particular cultures or societies and on the detailed description of their features. But where a larger aim has been pursued, it has been that of obtaining an understanding of the variation that is displayed at the level of sociocultural entities _per se_. That is, first, by cataloguing this variation as extensively as possible, and, second, by seeking patterns of association among particular variant features, with the ultimate aim of providing a systematic theoretical basis for the construction of typologies and for the allocation of cases to them.

Research and analysis in this vein did in fact hold a prominent position in sociology – and likewise in cultural and social anthropology – from the later nineteenth century through to the middle decades of the twentieth. As notable early examples, covering mainly tribal and early agrarian societies, one could take Spencer's (1873–1934) vast _Descriptive Sociology_, Tylor's (1889) efforts at demonstrating 'adhesions' among different forms of economic and familial institutions, and Hobhouse, Wheeler and Ginsberg's (1915) attempt essentially at widening the scope of Tylor's analyses while abandoning some of his more controversial evolutionary assumptions. In direct succession of this work, one could then place that of Murdock (1949) and

others on comparative social structure, using the Yale Human Relations Area Files – in the development of which Spencer was an
acknowledged influence (Murdock, 1965: ch. 2). And a further clear, if
not always fully recognised, continuity (although see Ginsberg, 1965)
can be traced between these earlier studies and much of the extensive
literature of the 1950s through to the 1970s on the transition from
'traditional' to 'modern' forms of social life (e.g. Hoselitz, 1952; Mead,
1953; Kerr et al., 1960; Lerner, 1964), whether focusing on change in
the cultures and social structures of local communities or of total
societies. In this latter regard, what could be taken as the final expression of the holistic paradigm in its most ambitious form came with
two books produced by Talcott Parsons towards the end of his remarkable sociological career. In these books, *Societies: Evolutionary and
Comparative Perspectives* (Parsons, 1966) and *The System of Modern
Societies* (Parsons, 1971), Parsons' explicit aim was 'to bring some
order' into 'the immense variety of types of society', understood as
'social systems' (1966: 1).[2]

The holistic 'containment' of the problem of variability has evident attractions, in particular in apparently staking out a quite specific sociological domain. Sociocultural entities can be represented
as realities *sui generis* that have to be studied as such rather than
in any way that involves 'reduction' to the individual level. And the
possibility is thus created of giving substance to classic programmatic
positions, such as those represented by Durkheim's (1895/1938: chs
I and V) assertion that social phenomena should be treated as 'things

---

[2] The irony has often been noted that Parsons' first major work (1937), in which his
ultimate concern was to develop a 'voluntaristic theory of action', opens with Crane
Brinton's rhetorical question, 'Who now reads Spencer?' Accepting that Spencer is
'dead', Parsons then poses as the key problem to be addressed that of 'Who killed him,
and how?' But in a way illustrative of sociologists' difficulties in letting go of the
holistic paradigm, Parsons eventually returned to a style of sociological thinking
remarkably close to that of Spencer – first, in adopting a version of functionalist
theory in *The Social System* (Parsons, 1952), and then in combining this with an
evolutionary perspective in the works cited in the text.

in themselves' and that 'social facts' can be explained only by reference to other social facts, or by Kroeber's (1917) insistence that
cultures should be regarded as non-reducible 'superorganisms' and
his and Robert Lowie's methodological maxim of *omnis cultura ex
cultura*.

However, a major problem does at the same time arise, and one
that over the recent past has led to increasing criticism of, or at all
events declining *de facto* commitment to, the holistic paradigm. What
is crucially at issue is the degree of variability that occurs *within*,
as well as among, sociocultural entities, whether total societies or
components thereof: that is, variability at the level of individuals.
For example, a question that immediately arises with the holistic
paradigm is that of what exactly is implied when a sociocultural entity
is said to be characterised by a particular institutional form – as, say,
of marriage and the family or of property ownership and inheritance.
Does this mean that this institutional form operates quite universally
within the population or subpopulation in question, or in a majority
of cases though with some exceptions, or perhaps represents only the
modal form with then a good deal of attendant variation? In sociological work in the style referred to previously, this kind of question
would appear to be more or less routinely evaded rather than seriously
addressed.

The holistic paradigm does in effect largely rely on the *assumption* that the entities that are taken as the units of analysis have a
high degree of internal homogeneity, resulting from belief and value
consensus and normative conformity. In Parsons' (1952) more specific formulation, norms deriving from shared beliefs and values are
'institutionalised' in social structure while at the same time they are
'internalised' in the development of individual personalities through
processes of enculturation and socialisation. Thus, for descriptive purposes, it is in turn supposed that knowledge of institutional forms can
in itself provide an adequate enough synopsis of prevailing patterns
of social action, with allowance being needed only for some, quite

limited, degree of individual variation that can be treated as recognised 'deviance'.[3]

Moreover, insofar as attempts are then made to account for features of sociocultural entities and the variation they display over place and time, theories can be adopted in which individual action carries little significance. Under these theories, which prove in fact almost invariably to depend on some form of functionalist explanatory logic, individuals serve as no more than the agents of the realisation of system 'imperatives' or 'exigencies', and in a way that renders their action – or, in effect, their socioculturally programmed behaviour – essentially epiphenomenal.

The very limited explanatory success that such theories have in practice achieved and the difficulties inherent in them in principle – in particular, their lack of adequate 'micro-foundations' (see Elster, 1979: ch. 5, 1983: ch. 2; Boudon, 1990; Coleman, 1990: ch. 1) – is certainly one source of the declining appeal of holism.[4] However, a yet more basic objection has been raised against the holistic paradigm, and one of more immediate relevance for present purposes: namely, that the extent to which it neglects individual variation occurring within sociocultural entities – or, in other words, the heterogeneity of their populations – is unacceptable; in the first place, simply on empirical grounds, and at a more basic level, in view

---

[3] At the London School of Economics in the later 1950s, when I was a graduate student in the Department of Sociology, Ginsberg was still an influential presence, and certain members of the department did indeed still *define* sociology as the study of social institutions, and viewed survey research carried out at the level of individuals as being of little sociological consequence.

[4] A basic and by now well-recognised problem of functionalist theories in sociology is that they provide little account of why individuals *should* act – perhaps to their disadvantage – in ways that are consistent with features of 'social systems' fulfilling the functions attributed to them. And in the absence of any such account, functionalist explanations must then rely on the existence of highly selective 'environments' such that, if a social system does not meet the functional imperatives that it faces, it will simply disappear and not therefore exist as a case going contrary to the theory. But, while there are instances of societies becoming 'extinct', there is little reason to suppose that in general a sufficiently powerful selectivity operates. Societies can, it seems, exist at very varying levels of effectiveness or success – whatever criteria may in these respects be envisaged.

of the seriously limited conception of the human individual that it entails.

To revert to the discussion of human sociality in Chapter 1, it could be argued that a further distinctive feature that it possesses is that, even though (or perhaps because?) developed to an exceptional degree, it does at the same time allow for *individuality* to a far greater extent than is found among all other species of 'social' animal. In particular, human individuals, even while involved in highly complex forms of social relations, are still able to conceive of interests and ends *as being their own, distinct and separate from those of the collectivities to which they belong* (see esp. Boyd and Richerson, 1999).[5] Thus, instead of seeking the approval of others through sociocultural conformity, they may pursue their own ends in diverse ways that disregard or knowingly contravene what might be taken as established beliefs, values and associated norms, and indeed in ways that may go beyond individual deviance and be aimed, perhaps in joint action with others, at the modification, reinterpretation or even radical change of norms.

It was essentially this point that was stressed by some of the earliest critics of the holistic paradigm in sociology in drawing attention to the 'over-socialised' conception of the individual actor and to the extreme 'social mould' theory of human nature that this paradigm implied. Authors such as Wrong (1961) and Homans (1964) observed that while processes of socialisation are indeed fundamental in making individuals 'human' in the sense of endowing them with uniquely human attributes, these processes do *not* thereby entail that within

---

[5] The point is entertainingly brought out in the animated film, *Antz*. The deviant – because anthropomorphic – ant, Z-4195, bitterly complains (in the voice of Woody Allen), 'It's this whole gung-ho superorganism thing that I *just can't get*. I try, but I just don't get it. What is it, I'm supposed to do everything for the colony and ... what about *my* needs?' It is, though, important to note that, to adopt Sen's (1986: 7–8) terminology, 'self-goal choice' as opposed to 'other-goal choice' need not be selfish in the sense of being concerned only with 'self-welfare goals'. It can be altruistic even while normatively deviant – as, say, with Robin Hood, stealing from the rich to give to the poor.

particular cultures or subcultures, societies or groups, individuals become essentially alike in the beliefs, values and norms that they accept or in the ends that they pursue (and see further Boudon, 2003a). To the contrary, a high degree of variability in these respects is always to be expected. In later work, Wrong (1999) has emphasised in this connection the importance of diversity in individual life-courses. At the same time as being involved in 'recurrent webs' of social relations, individuals, he argues, are still found, even in what may appear to be highly stable and homogenous sociocultural contexts, to have very different personal histories as a result of the many different factors that can impinge on their lives, including quite chance events (see further Chapter 4).

Research in many different fields of sociology could by now be regarded as providing ample support for questioning of the holistic paradigm on the lines indicated. Consider, as just one example, research into religious or political beliefs and values and their expression in forms of religious or political action. This research reveals vast individual variation. And while analyses that include a range of indicators of individuals' subcultural or social group affiliations are indeed able to bring out systematic aspects of this variation – or, in other words, probabilistic population-level regularities of major sociological interest (see e.g. Evans and De Graaf, 2013) – it is still the case that *only a quite modest part of the total variation is in this way accounted for*; and, it is important to note, *far less* than would have to be expected on the basis of holistic assumptions (see further Chapter 7).

Another way of putting the central issue that arises here would be to say that within the holistic paradigm the attempt is made – but has not in fact succeeded – to 'endogenise' the ends of individual action and the beliefs and values from which these ends derive. In mainstream economics the exogeneity of tastes or preferences has been generally accepted. But sociologists have shown a reluctance to take up an analogous position. Thus, even in early Parsons (1937: 58–65 esp.), the assumption that he identified in the work of the utilitarians and the classical economists of 'the randomness of ends' was, for him, a major shortcoming, and one which, if correct, would, he believed, render the idea of social order highly problematic. For if a society is to cohere, the ends that its individual members pursue cannot be merely random but have, to a substantial degree, to be integrated through normative congruence at the institutional and individual levels. However, the attempts at endogenising ends that were made by Parsons in his later work progressed little beyond the programmatic stage, and the same limitation would apply to those that have been subsequently made by others (see Goldthorpe, 2007: vol. 1, ch. 8), while human societies would, as a matter of fact, appear capable of existing, and persisting, in a far less integrated condition than adherents of the holistic paradigm have to suppose.

What has then to be recognised, if only pragmatically, is that even if the idea of the randomness of individual ends is an exaggeration in that these ends and the ways in which they are formed and pursued are socioculturally structured to some extent, this extent is still quite limited; and also that, as Elster (1997: 753) has observed, why in fact people have the particular ends – the goals, desires, tastes or preferences – that they do remains perhaps 'the most important unsolved problem in the social sciences'. Indeed, what has yet further to be recognised is the possibility that this is a problem that may never be solved insofar as the choice of ends represents the ultimate indeterminism in human social life. At all events, for the time being at least, it is difficult to see that sociology has any alternative than to follow economics and to take individual ends as the basic 'givens' of analysis.[6]

---

[6] It is, however, important to note that, from a sociological standpoint, there are no grounds whatever for taking the further step, as proposed by economists such as Stigler and Becker (1977), of treating ends, or 'tastes', as being stable over time and similar across individuals, the purpose of which – highly implausible – assumptions is simply to allow all economic analysis to then be done by reference to changes in prices and incomes.

From the foregoing, major implications for sociological inquiry do therefore follow. First, since the states and behaviour of individuals *cannot* be adequately read off simply from a knowledge of institutional forms, it is necessary that individuals and their actions *should be studied directly*. And second, they have to be studied through methods that are fit for purpose in two different respects. These methods have, on the one hand, to be capable of accommodating and revealing, rather than in effect suppressing, the full extent of the variability that exists within sociocultural entities at the individual level; and they have, on the other hand, to be capable of allowing reliable empirical demonstrations to be made of any – probabilistic – regularities that may be emergent from this variability. In other words, what is required is a methodological approach to both data collection and data analysis through which typological thinking can be superseded by population thinking.

In order to give a more specific expression of the issues that arise here, I turn to a now rather little discussed but still, I believe, highly revealing passage from the history of cultural and social anthropology that has its origins in the work of Bronisław Malinowski. In his book *Crime and Custom in Savage Society*, Malinowski raised a direct challenge to prevailing holistic orthodoxy. In particular, he questioned the view – which he associated with Durkheim, Hobhouse, Lowie and others – that 'in primitive societies the individual is completely dominated by the group', that 'he obeys the commands of his community, its traditions, its public opinion, its decrees with a slavish, fascinated, passive obedience', and that 'he is hemmed in on every side by the customs of his people' (Malinowski, 1926: 3–4, 10). On the basis of his fieldwork among the Trobriand Islanders, Malinowski sought to show that this view was far too extreme. While the Trobrianders were well aware of the social constraints bearing on them, they also had a clear understanding of their own interests and of how these might conflict with those of their community and with its legal and customary norms. Consequently, customary norms, especially, were subject not only to a wide range of interpretation but often also to quite systematic evasion, as individuals knowingly and openly pursued their own ends. With rather splendid irony, Malinowski could then ask whether tribal or clan solidarity is 'such an overwhelming and universal force' or 'whether the heathen can be as self-seeking and self-interested as any Christian' (1926: ix).

Moreover, and with yet wider-reaching implications, Malinowski had a methodological point to make. He warned of the shortcomings of 'verandah' or 'hearsay' ethnography, in which main reliance is placed on 'informants' rather than on the direct and sustained observation of the people under study – in the way that he himself pioneered. Informants, Malinowski held, tended to tell their questioners far more about prevailing norms than about what people actually thought and did (1926: 120–1). The danger then was – especially under holistic assumptions – that the two things would be inadequately distinguished.

Subsequently, one of Malinowski's most faithful and talented students, Audrey Richards (1957), insightfully elaborated on what had to follow from his substantive and methodological arguments together. She emphasised the way in which in reports on his fieldwork Malinowski always presented extensive data on individuals as well as on groups and on variation in individual behaviour as well as on conformity – implying here, it would seem safe to say, a contrast with Malinowski's contemporary and great rival, A. R. Radcliffe-Brown, in whose analyses, as another of Malinowski's students remarked, 'people...are conspicuous by their absence' (Kaberry, 1957: 88).[7] Then – most significantly for present purposes – Richards went on to spell out what this must mean for research practice that aimed to go beyond – while still maintaining the inherent logic of – the advances in

---

[7] Malinowski and Radcliffe-Brown are often regarded as the twin pioneers of functionalist analysis in sociology. But their functionalisms were of very different kinds. Malinowski was concerned primarily with the functions of cultural practices and social institutions in meeting individuals' biological and psychological needs, rather than in maintaining societal needs of integration and stability. For a revealing account of their contrasting positions in this and other respects, see Kuper (1973: chs 1, 2).

fieldwork that Malinowski himself had made. Her conclusion was that 'Once individual variation in human behaviour was admitted, and it had to be admitted, then anthropologists... were bound to the use of quantitative data'. Such data had to be derived from the appropriate sampling of individuals in the populations studied, so that the extent of variability could be adequately treated, and had to be analysed through the application of various statistical techniques, so that possible regularities within this variability could be revealed (Richards, 1957: 28–30).

Richards was not in fact alone in seeing the radical implications of Malinowski's work – the implications of what Leach (1957: 119) described as his transformation of ethnography 'from the museum study of items of custom into the sociological study of systems of action'. However, for those committed to the holistic paradigm – or, as Richards significantly puts it to 'social typologies' – these implications appeared seriously threatening. What gave cause for greatest concern was not in itself the requirement for the use of quantitative methods, for such methods had been quite widely – even if not always very convincingly – applied within the holistic paradigm in the attempts, previously noted, at the construction of typologies.[8] Far more disturbing was that a concern with individual variability but at the same time with emergent population regularities, as might be demonstrated through quantitative methods, called into question the practice of typological thinking, and indeed its very point. The

---

[8] For example, Hobhouse, Wheeler and Ginsberg (1915) regarded their work as 'an essay in correlation', although the methods of correlation they applied were very crude, even by the standards of the time. Murdock (1949) made use of Yule's coefficient of association, Q, and of significance testing. It might, however, be added that a basic statistical difficulty raised in work of the kind in question is that the results of the analyses carried out rest largely on the assumption of independent observations, whereas Galton (1889b) pointed out, already in commentary on Tylor, that this assumption is very questionable. It could well be that associations among institutional features derive not only from internal functional requirements but also from processes of diffusion across cultures and societies. The 'Galton problem' would seem never to have been entirely resolved in comparative research within the holistic paradigm.

kind of criticism that was most often directed against Malinowski amounted in effect to the charge that his research revealed too much. Thus, as Richards (1957: 28) recounts, Evans-Pritchard regarded Malinowski's analyses as being 'overloaded with (cultural) reality', while Gluckman characterised his field data as 'too complex for comparative work'. But, given their commitment to typological thinking, what such critics were unable – or unwilling – to recognise was the possibility that, with population thinking and associated methods of data collection and analysis, individual variability *and* sociocultural regularity could be treated together.

As a coda to this illustration, it should be said that neither Malinowski's work itself nor Richards' attempt to bring out the need for quantitative methods in accommodating individual variability would seem to have resulted in any immediate questioning of the holistic paradigm within anthropology.[9] And insofar as its hold has more recently been weakened, a probably more powerful influence can be identified: that is, the increasing *historical* study of societies previously supposed to be of a kind 'without history' (see Carrithers, 1992: ch. 2 esp.). Such research has demonstrated in another way that to seek to understand even tribal or peasant societies as 'internally homogenous and externally distinctive and bounded objects' (Wolf, 1982: 6) is not a viable approach, and that such societies have to be recognised as subject to division, instability and often turbulent change, internally as well as externally induced. Perhaps most striking in this regard is Jan Vansina's work on the history of Equatorial Africa and his

---

[9] In the post-war years, Richards' position in British social anthropology became strangely marginal – even in her own department at Cambridge, where, during the 1960s, I came to know her. Few systematic attempts were made within anthropology to apply quantitative methods to deal with variability at the individual level – the most important perhaps being in research carried out at the Rhodes-Livingstone Institute at Lusaka on the position of African migrant workers in the urban centres of the Copperbelt. See, for example, the work of Clyde Mitchell (1969) – from whom I later learned much when he became a colleague at Nuffield College, Oxford. Interestingly, Kuper (1973: 188) comments that this research was accompanied by a movement towards 'methodological individualism' – the basis of the individualistic as opposed to the holistic paradigm in sociology, as discussed in Chapter 3.

critique of the practice of taking tribes as the units of analysis on the assumptions that they were 'perennial' and of 'almost indeterminate age', that their members held, traditionally, to 'the same beliefs and practices' and that 'every tribe differed from its neighbours' (Vansina, 1990: 19–20). Against this, Vansina stresses 'ceaseless change' among the populations of the region – including change even in tribal and ethnic identities – and urges that rather than 'tradition' being taken to imply lack of change, traditions should be understood as 'processes', dependent on individual autonomy, that 'must continually change to remain alive' (1990: 257–60).[10]

In sociology, too, it may be noted, historical research – often drawing on quantitative archival material – has provided a basis for telling criticism of the holistic paradigm and of typological thinking, most notably in regard to the idea of traditional subcultures and communities. For example, Thernstrom (1964) showed that Newburyport, the 'Yankee City' studied by Lloyd Warner and his associates in the 1930s, was not the relatively insulated, well-integrated and static community that they suggested (see esp. Warner and Lunt, 1941, 1948), but rather one that had experienced substantial in- and out-migration, recurrent social conflict and high levels of social mobility.[11] Similarly, Baines and Johnson (1999) have observed that the supposedly traditional working class community that Young and Willmott (1957) claimed to find in Bethnal Green in the 1950s must, if it existed at all, have been a relatively recent product of post-war circumstances, since in the interwar years this area of east London was a quite unstable one, characterised by high rates of mobility, both residential and occupational.

---

[10] I am indebted to my colleague, John Darwin, for drawing my attention to Vansina's remarkable work.

[11] It should be said that Warner and most of his associates were in fact social anthropologists by training, primarily under the influence of Radcliffe-Brown, but were committed to bringing anthropological research methods and theory into sociology and opted therefore to work primarily in modern societies.

However, within sociology at large, the holistic paradigm could be said to have lost its sway chiefly as a result of its quite manifest inappropriateness to societies within which the degree of individual variability, and thus of population heterogeneity, is impossible to ignore – at all events in the actual conduct of research. As will later be shown, in the transition – slow and often more implicit than explicit – from typological to population thinking that is now in train, a crucial driving force has been the inescapable need for quantitative methods of both data collection and analysis through which this variability and heterogeneity can be accommodated and in various ways exploited.

3   The individualistic paradigm

In sociology, understood as a population science, an 'individualistic' rather than a holistic paradigm of inquiry is required because of the high degree of variability existing at the individual level, and, further, because individual action, while subject to sociocultural conditioning and constraints, has to be accorded causal primacy in human social life, on account of the degree of autonomy that it retains.

Boudon (1990; see also 1987) provides a clear statement in principle of the case for an individualistic, as opposed to a holistic, paradigm of inquiry in sociology, acknowledging its origins in the work of Max Weber (see esp. 1922/1968: ch. 1). Boudon emphasises that the individualistic paradigm does not involve 'an atomistic view of societies', nor a denial of the *sui generis* reality of sociocultural phenomena and of the ways in which they may motivate, constrain or otherwise pattern individual action (1990: 57). In other words, there is no claim of *ontological* individualism: that is, no claim that only individuals *exist* (or, to quote Mrs Thatcher, that 'there is no such thing as society'). Rather, the argument is for *methodological* individualism (Popper, 1945: vol. 2, ch. 14; 1957: ch. IV): that is, for the position that sociocultural phenomena have themselves to be accounted for, in the last analysis, in terms of individual action. While it may be entirely reasonable for the purposes of many sociological inquiries to take certain such phenomena as givens, rather than as the explananda of immediate interest, it still remains the case that if they were to be explained, this could only be by reference to individual action and to its present or past, intended or unintended, direct or indirect consequences (see Hedström and Swedberg, 1998a; Elster, 2007: ch. 1).[1]

---

[1] An analogous situation, pointed out to me by David Cox, is that in many investigations in physics it is not necessary to go down to the quantum level – although this

The principle of methodological individualism is one that might well be taken as 'trivially true' (Elster, 1989: 13). Difficulty in accepting it would in fact appear to arise either because of a failure to see that methodological individualism does not entail ontological individualism or because of an insistence that individual action is always influenced by the social conditions under which it occurs – a claim that could also be regarded as trivially true, but without being in any way damaging to methodological individualism.[2] The crucial issue to be addressed is that of where else in human social life actual causal capacity could lie if not with the action of individuals, under whatever conditions it may be taken. The main, if not the only, form of sociological theory that has sought to dispense with this capacity is that of functionalism, following the logic of explanation set out in Chapter 2, in which individual action is in effect reduced to epiphenomenal, socioculturally programmed behaviour. But, as was further observed, while functionalism represents the main theoretical resource of the holistic paradigm, it can, in its actual application, claim very little in the way of explanatory success.

What follows from acceptance of the individualistic paradigm is then that norms and their embodiment in cultural traditions or social institutions cannot serve as a satisfactory 'bottom line' in sociological explanations (see further Boudon, 2003a). Such explanations have to be grounded in accounts of individual action; and where the influence of social norms is invoked, the further questions must always be raised of why it is *these* norms, rather than others, that are in place, and of why individuals conform with them – insofar as they do – rather than deviating from them or openly challenging them. No explanatory logic can be thought adequate that requires that the actions

level would indeed have to be resorted to if a 'rock bottom' explanation of all the phenomena involved were to be required.

[2] It is also possible that methodological individualism may be opposed because it is taken to imply some commitment to individualism as an economic or political creed. But as Weber (1922/1968: 18) himself observed, 'It is a tremendous misunderstanding to think that an "individualistic" method should involve what is in any conceivable sense an individualistic system of values'.

of individuals should, as it were, follow from some pre-ordained script.[3]

However, for present purposes, what needs to be more clearly brought out are the *sources* of the autonomy in human action that necessitates and underwrites the individualistic paradigm. The evolved capacity of human individuals, as earlier noted, to conceive of ends that are their own, as distinct from those of the collectivities to which they belong, is one such source. But an essential complement has also to be recognised insofar as the link between ends and action is concerned: that is, humans' further evolved capacity for what might be called *informed choice*. This capacity derives from humans' distinctive mental ability – in which language would appear to have a crucial role – to *prefigure* actions that they might take in pursuit of their ends, given the information they have about the situations in which they find themselves. Other animals, even primates, appear to live in an eternal present or to be able to 'plan ahead' in only quite limited ways: chimpanzees cannot learn to tend fires. In contrast, humans, one might say, can readily think in the future perfect tense. They can mentally rehearse not just one but a number of different courses of action that they might follow in a certain situation, and are in turn in a position to assess and evaluate in advance the likely consequences of acting in one way rather than another (see e.g. Dennett, 1995: ch. 13; Dunbar, 2000, 2004: 64–9, 104–7; Gärdenfors, 2006: chs 2–5). And what may of course be at issue here is setting the advantages offered, in relation to given ends, by some form of normatively deviant or perhaps normatively innovative action against the disadvantages of engaging in it.[4]

---

[3] In this respect, Boudon (1990: 41) illuminatingly contrasts his own position with that of his compatriot, Pierre Bourdieu, who, through his application – or, it could be held, misapplication – of the Thomist notion of *habitus*, in effect supposes an over-socialised conception of the individual actor yet more extreme than that against which, in a mainly American context, Wrong and Homans earlier objected. See further Boudon (2003b: 140–8).

[4] The work in cognitive and evolutionary psychology referred to in the sources cited helps remedy a major weakness in the critiques of 'over-socialised' conceptions of

This capacity for informed choice can then be seen as in turn implying some form of rationality in action: that is, that which operates when individuals actually make choices among the possibilities open to them. As Runciman (1998: 15) has put it, '... there is every reason to suppose that the human mind has been programmed by natural selection to calculate the trade-off between the costs and the benefits of one course of action rather than another'.[5] And, as will later be seen, it is on an appreciation of this 'rationality of everyday life' that the individualistic paradigm primarily draws in seeking to account for the individual action and interaction which it treats as being – in the short term or the long, intentionally or unintentionally, directly or indirectly – the generative force of sociocultural phenomena.

Exactly how the rationality of everyday life operates is the subject of much current research and debate. On one important point, though, a consensus could be said to exist. It would be generally accepted, on empirical grounds, that the kind of rationality

the human actor advanced by Wrong and Homans – that is, that the psychological foundations of these critiques were questionable as well as being quite contradictory, Wrong appealing to a Freudian theory of instincts and Homans to a rather crude behaviourism. Sociologists have often reacted in a very negative way to positions taken up by evolutionary psychologists in particular – as, for example, to that of Tooby and Cosmides (1992) in their attack on 'the standard social science model' of the human individual as implying a 'blank slate' (see also Pinker, 2002). This attack can in fact be understood as one focused specifically on the psychological assumptions underlying the holistic paradigm and, on this interpretation, is well-conceived. But a problem arises from the authors' failure then to make the distinction between ontological and methodological individualism. A commitment to the latter in no way entails underwriting their very unfortunate claim that 'what mostly remains, once you have removed from the human world everything internal to individuals, is the air between them' (Tooby and Cosmides, 1992: 47; see further Goldthorpe, 2007: vol. 1, 180–3).

[5] Interestingly, Dunbar (2004: 64–6) suggests that the highly developed theory of mind that underlies human ultra-sociality may be an emergent property of this more basic capacity for informed choice in that the kind of reasoning that the latter entails could provide the platform for the understanding of other minds: 'I use my experience of my own mental processes to imagine how someone else's mind might work.' This suggestion is in line with well-known arguments in both philosophy and anthropology that it is the idea of rationality that provides the essential *passe partout* into other minds and in turn into other cultures (see e.g. Hollis, 1987: ch. 1).

in question is clearly different from that typically assumed in mainstream economics – the social science within which an individualistic paradigm of inquiry has hitherto been most dominant. That is to say, it is not a 'demonic' or 'hyper' rationality that in effect requires actors to possess unlimited information and calculating power.[6] Rather, some form of subjective or bounded rationality is envisaged that aims at good enough, or 'satisficing', rather than optimising, outcomes (Simon, 1982, 1983) and that can operate on the basis of only quite limited information and calculation alike, and under conditions that are in any event often characterised by a high degree of uncertainty.

Versions of such rationality that can be regarded as to a large extent complementary have been outlined from both psychological (e.g. Gigerenzer and Selten, 1999; Augier and March, 2004; Gigerenzer, 2008) and sociological (e.g. Boudon, 1996, 2003a; Blossfeld and Prein, 1998; Goldthorpe, 2007: vol. 1, chs 6–8) standpoints. In the former case, the emphasis is on the procedural, 'inside-the-skin' aspects of everyday rationality: for example, on individuals' use in decision-making processes of 'fast and frugal' heuristics – ones that can be applied quickly and with relatively little information but that have been found to give generally positive outcomes in particular situations or, that is, in the environments in which they have evolved.[7] In the

---

[6] 'Demonic' refers here to the demon envisaged by Laplace (1814/1951) whose intelligence transcends all informational and calculating constraints and for whom nothing is uncertain and the future is as apparent as the past. Economists sometimes claim that much theoretical work has in fact been carried out on information costs and limits on calculation and on their consequences. But how far this does then feed into the treatment of decision-making in applied economics research may be questioned. For example, consider the following statement made in a paper on parental decision-making in regard to the financial support to be given to children's education: 'With smoothly functioning capital markets, parents equate the market interest rate on borrowing with the present value of the marginal return to investing in offspring' (Blanden et al., 2010: p. 30). They do, do they?

[7] It is important to distinguish the body of psychological research referred to here from that of the 'heuristics and biases' programme associated with Kahneman and Tversky (see e.g. Kahneman, 2011). The emphasis in the latter is on how and why individuals' choices and actions often violate established principles of logic and

latter case, the emphasis is on situational aspects *per se*: that is, on the way in which individuals can be understood as acting, if not optimally from a 'demonic' standpoint, then still appropriately for the attainment of their ends – for 'good reasons' (Boudon, 2003a) – once features of the conditions under which they are required to act, such as resource, informational or time constraints, are taken into account.

In this body of work, it should be emphasised, it is fully recognised that informed, subjectively rational choice may itself often lead to conformity with established norms and practices. For example, in many situations 'Do what the others do' may indeed serve as a good fast and frugal heuristic (Gigerenzer and Todd, 1999; see also Richerson and Boyd, 2005: 119–26) – one that saves on the costs of individual experimentation and learning and that, for so long as it helps individuals in pursuing their ends, may be adopted as a matter, more or less, of habit. And it is further recognised that norms, whether informal or institutionalised, may be quite rationally accepted and followed: for example, as a means of overcoming both relatively simple co-ordination problems (in Britain, drive on the left – almost everywhere else, on the right) and, if with some amount of free-riding, more difficult 'public goods' problems (see Ostrom, 1990, 2000). However, what is questioned (e.g. Edgerton, 1992; Boyd and Richerson, 1999) is the supposition that prevailing norms are always and necessarily 'adaptive'. Thus, where previously stable situations are disrupted or quite new situations arise, the 'Do what the others do' heuristic and unreflective and unconditional norm-following may appear increasingly ineffective as regards individuals' attainment of their ends (Laland, 1999). And what is then all-important is that the

probability – with the normative superiority of these principles being taken as given. In contrast, in the work of Gigerenzer and his associates especially, the idea of 'content-blind' norms of rationality is questioned, and the emphasis is on how fast and frugal heuristics can, under conditions to which they are adapted, match or even outdo demonic rationality in helping actors to achieve what they would themselves regard as positive outcomes (see further Gigerenzer, 2008: ch. 1; Berg and Gigerenzer, 2010).

individuals concerned have the cognitive resources to respond by conceiving of alternative courses of action, including perhaps ones that are of a normatively deviant or innovative kind, and by making informed choices among them.

In sum, attempts at providing a basis for the individualistic paradigm in sociology at the level of action entail a rejection of *Homo economicus*, driven by a demonic rationality, in favour of an understanding of the actor more securely grounded in the nature of *Homo sapiens sapiens* and guided by what Gigerenzer (2008) has called 'rationality for mortals'. Nonetheless, these attempts still result in an understanding of the actor that is very different from, and far more developed than, that found within the holistic paradigm. Rather than individuals being treated as to a large degree the creatures of the sociocultural entities within which they are born and live – in the extreme as sociocultural puppets – their capacities for envisaging their own ends and for choosing, in some sense rationally, among different possible means of pursuing them are underlined. It is these capacities that endow individuals with a significant degree of autonomy from their sociocultural conditioning and in virtue of which the individualistic paradigm is required and validated.

Moreover, in this perspective, one further significant advantage of the individualistic paradigm becomes apparent: it allows, perhaps somewhat paradoxically, for a better appreciation of the nature of *constraints on individual action*. Within the holistic paradigm, the focus is on normative constraints. However, since it is also supposed that, through processes of enculturation and socialisation, norms that are in various ways institutionalised tend also to be internalised in individual personalities, the distinction between constraint and choice in individual action becomes blurred, if not lost. Action is in effect reduced to normatively shaped social behaviour. It was in fact such a reduction that prompted the old joke, directed against the work of Parsons and usually attributed to the economist James Duesenberry, that, while economics is all about choices, sociology is all about why there are no choices to be made.

In contrast, within the individualistic paradigm the possibility is readily accommodated that social norms may be subjectively experienced *as* constraints: that is, as imposing external limitations on individuals' action that are not grounded in beliefs and values in which they themselves share. And, further, it becomes easier to see that to centre attention on normative constraints on action is in any event seriously limiting. Other constraints exist, of at least comparable importance, that are of a *non*-normative kind: that is, what David Lockwood, in an early critique of Parsons, labelled as 'factual' constraints (Lockwood, 1956; see further Lockwood, 1992: 93–7 esp.). These are constraints that do not depend on any commonalty in beliefs and values but simply express brute inequalities among individuals and groups in their command over resources – economic, political and other – and thus in their social advantage and power. In this way, individuals' opportunities for action, or, that is, the range of choices realistically open to them, are systematically and often extremely differentiated.

From this point of view, it is then scarcely surprising that the treatment of structured social inequalities in resources – or, in other words, of social stratification – has always constituted a serious problem within the holistic paradigm: specifically, that of how social stratification should be reconciled with what is supposed about the internal homogeneity of the sociocultural entities that are taken as the units of analysis and about their degree of integration.[8] From the

---

[8] The most common approach to the problem, followed by Parsons (1940), among others (e.g. Davis and Moore, 1945), has been to treat social stratification as being itself normatively sanctioned and generally accepted as a necessary response to functional exigencies: that is, those of ensuring the allocation of the most able individuals to those roles most important for 'system maintenance' and of ensuring their motivation to perform at a high level in these roles. Such theories of social stratification have, however, been subjected to a wide range of both conceptually and empirically grounded critique (for an early example, see Tumin, 1953) and have by now little currency. An alternative approach characteristic of Marxist-inspired *fonctionnalisme noir*, as opposed to Parsons' *fonctionnalisme rose* – to take up Raymond Aron's nice distinction – has been to regard acceptance of social stratification as indicative of a social system, the integration and maintenance of which derive from the ideological, as well as economic and political, domination of inferior by superior classes.

standpoint of the individualistic paradigm, in contrast, social stratification and the operation of the non-normative constraints that follow from it present no difficulties. They are regarded as further major factors increasing the heterogeneity of human populations and creating variability in human social life – in this case, variability, one might say, in life-chances that is *prior to* variability in life-choices. And in this way, the need for sociology to be based – to return again to Mayr's distinction – on population thinking rather than on typological thinking is re-emphasised.

The argument of this chapter so far has been somewhat abstract, and in order to bring out more clearly what is entailed, it may be helpful in conclusion to provide some more concrete illustration of its central points. This can be done by reference to one of the most remarkable processes of social change that is evident in the contemporary Western world: that is, the quite rapid erosion, from the 1960s onwards, of beliefs, values and related social norms sanctioning marriage as the basis of sexual relationships and of child-bearing and child-rearing, and the corresponding increase in the numbers of individuals opting for non-marital cohabitation and family formation.

It may first of all be noted that analyses of this process (e.g. Nazio and Blossfeld, 2003; Nazio, 2008) show how it began with a relatively small increase in the numbers deviating from prevailing norms – but including, to use Merton's (1957: ch. IV) distinction, not only pragmatic 'innovators' but also 'rebels'; that is, individuals opposed to what they regarded as 'bourgeois conventions' and whose quite open entry into cohabitation would appear to have created a significant demonstration effect.

The diffusion of the practice then gathered pace as members of successive birth cohorts could not only observe more examples of cohabitation among their coevals but, further, became increasingly aware of the cost–benefit advantages that it could afford – even if still to some, declining, extent regarded as deviant – and especially so in a period in which economic opportunities and constraints were being substantially reshaped. Women's labour market opportunities were widening, but many men and women alike were experiencing greater uncertainty in their early working lives (Blossfeld and Hofmeister, 2006; Blossfeld, Mills and Bernhardi, 2006). In these circumstances, entry into cohabitation was often found more attractive – as a matter, one could say, of informed choice – than the alternatives of either marrying or remaining unattached. Through cohabitation, long-term commitment could be delayed until some measure of worklife security had been achieved without incurring the costs of sexual isolation or promiscuity; and at the same time, the advantages of pooled resources and economies of scale in living together could be gained (Oppenheimer, 1994, 1997; Mills, Blossfeld and Klijzing, 2005; Bukodi, 2012).

Such analyses of the decline of marriage and the rise of cohabitation do then well illustrate the potential force of individual autonomy as against prevailing norms in response to changing conditions of action. In addition, though, they also serve to bring out one other point of relevance for present purposes. They show that when previously well-established social norms are undermined by processes of individuals' informed choice, neither movement towards some new normative consensus nor radical disorder necessarily follows.

In most societies, the increase in cohabitation would appear, so far at least, to have been associated simply with greater *normative diversity*. Previously dominant norms still retain some degree of influence alongside new norms. For example, those individuals who have a religious affiliation are more likely than those who do not to enter into marriage without prior cohabitation; and they are also more likely, if they do cohabit, to move to marriage at some point, as, for example, following the conception or birth of a child (Manting, 1996; Nazio, 2008). Thus, one might say, men and women have created greater degrees of freedom than before to realise the differing ideas and ideals that they would wish to live by; or, as Thornton, Axinn and Xie (2007: 73) have aptly put it, individuals 'have reclaimed from the community and larger social system control over crucial elements of the union-formation process'. Lesthaeghe (2010: 213–16) would in fact see the increase in cohabitation as but one aspect of a 'second demographic transition', which involves 'an overhaul of the normative structure' regarding not only marriage and partnership but also sexual relations and child-bearing and -rearing, and in which autonomous 'individual choices' and 'utility' evaluations have prevailed over 'social group adherence'.[9]

However, changes of the kind in question need not be taken to imply that social order is then reduced, or at all events not in the sense of there being less regularity in social life. Individuals pursuing their own ends through processes of informed choice can also be a source of regularities at a population level: that is, through individuals making similar choices in similar situations (see Goldthorpe, 2007: vol. 1, ch. 6). And further in this regard, the effects of non-normative as well as of normative constraints in patterning social action can take on large importance. Thus, in the case of cohabitation, a major non-normative constraint on its diffusion is that imposed by the mundane matter of housing costs. For example, it has been shown (Nazio and Blossfeld, 2003; Nazio, 2008) that in countries such as Italy and Spain, where a shortage of low-cost housing exists, many young couples, especially in lower social strata, who would wish to cohabit are in fact prevented from so doing and are forced to stay in their family homes simply out of economic necessity.

High levels of belief and value consensus and of normative conformity should not then be regarded as the only sources of regularity in social life. At the same time, though, a further conclusion can be drawn from both the general argument of this chapter and the specific illustration of it that has been given, which has direct consequences for what is to follow.

---

[9] I would, though, stress that one does not have to suppose, as Lesthaeghe would seem inclined to do, that what is entailed here is some unilinear and irreversible movement – as, say, from 'tradition' to 'modernity'. It is quite possible to envisage that, again under changing conditions, individual action might lead to the re-emergence of a situation of increased normative consensus and conformity.

Where individuals seek in informed ways to pursue their own ends under conditions created by possibly quite diverse normative commitments and also by non-normative constraints that limit possible choices in very varying degrees, the regularities in action and in its outcomes that emerge at a population level are likely to be generated in more complex ways than would be expected under holistic assumptions. And this fact has then direct implications for the difficulties involved, to revert to the discussion of Chapter 1, in making these regularities both visible and transparent. Where sociological analysis starts out from the idea of populations and subpopulations, rather than from that of sociocultural entities considered at more micro- or macro-levels, what must follow is an awareness of human society as being, so to speak, far more loosely textured than it would appear under the holistic paradigm, while at the same time having a far more intricate weave. And such an awareness in turn reinforces what was said at the end of Chapter 2 about the requirements that methods of data collection and analysis must meet if population regularities are to be adequately established and described, and is further relevant in determining the appropriate form of explanation for these regularities.

The issues that arise here are ones that will be central to subsequent chapters, with the exception of Chapter 4, which represents a necessary excursus in order to make the case that it *is* probabilistic population regularities that constitute the proper explananda of sociology.

4 Population regularities as basic explananda

For sociology understood as a population science, the basic explananda are probabilistic population regularities rather than singular events or events that are grouped together under some rubric but without any adequate demonstration of the underlying regularities that would warrant such a grouping.

Elster (2007: 9) has argued that 'The main task of the social sciences is to explain social phenomena' and that 'The basic type of explanandum is an *event*.' From the standpoint of sociology as a population science, Elster's argument needs to be qualified in one important respect. The events with which sociology is concerned are ones of a certain kind: that is, events that can be shown to occur within a given population or subpopulation *with some degree of regularity.*

Most of the explananda, or 'puzzles', for sociology that Elster (2007: 1–5) suggests by way of illustrating his argument do in fact relate to regularities in events: for example, 'Why are poor people less likely to emigrate?' and 'Why does an individual vote in elections when his or her vote is virtually certain to have no effect on the outcome?' However, some further instances that he gives refer to singular events: for example, 'Why did President Chirac call early elections in 1997, only to lose his majority in parliament?'[1] And, more

---

[1] Elster also gives examples which, while referring to singular events, are, it seems, to be understood as particular instances of regularities. For example, 'Why did none of thirty-eight bystanders call the police when Kitty Genovese was beaten to death?' (Kitty Genovese was a New York bar manager who was murdered while on her way home in the early hours of the morning one day in 1964.) What, one supposes, Elster is concerned with here is the so-called 'bystander effect', much discussed in the social-psychological literature, which could be formulated in general terms as follows: 'The probability of individuals providing help or taking other action in apparently emergency situations varies inversely with the numbers of those present.' Actually, the Genovese case is not a well-documented instance of this effect (Manning, Levine and Collins, 2007).

importantly for present purposes, there are other authors (e.g. Brady, Collier and Seawright, 2006; Mahoney and Goertz, 2006; Mahoney and Larkin Terrie, 2008) who recognise more explicitly than Elster the distinction between regularities in events and singular events and who still maintain that the social sciences should be as much concerned with explaining the latter as the former.

To see why difficulties arise when distinctive, singular events, rather than regularities in events, are taken as sociological explananda, it is necessary to consider further the role of *chance* in social life. In this regard, a distinction between two different understandings, or usages, of 'chance' in a scientific context, which has been proposed by the biologist Jacques Monod (1970), is of value: that is, the distinction between 'operational' and 'essential' chance.

Monod observes that chance is invoked in an operational sense when, in dealing with certain phenomena, a probabilistic approach is, in practice, the only methodologically feasible one – even if, in principle, a deterministic approach might be applicable. It is then chance in this operational sense that is basic to the idea of a population science as understood by Neyman. The infeasibility is accepted of seeking to account in a deterministic way for the states and behaviour of all individuals making up a population, whether because they are inherently indeterminate or simply because of the degree of complexity of the determination involved. Nonetheless, the possibility still exists of – to revert to Hacking's phrase – 'the taming of chance' by establishing regularities of a probabilistic kind at the aggregate, population level, and by then seeking explanations of these regularities as resulting from causal processes or mechanisms operating at the individual level which incorporate chance.

In contrast, essential chance is, for Monod, a far more radical idea and applies where some outcome results from the *intersection* of two or more quite independent series of events (see Hacking, 1990: 12). In the example Monod (1970: 127–31) gives, Dr Dupont goes out on an emergency call but, as he passes by a building where repairs are being carried out, roofer Dubois drops his hammer, which falls on Dr

Dupont's head and kills him. Even if the two series of events are themselves seen as in some way determined, their independence means that their joint outcome has still to be understood as a *'coïncidence absolue'*.[2]

Now, in human social life the operation of essential chance might seem pervasive. Individuals do often find themselves, like Dr Dupont, in the wrong place at the wrong time, or, more happily, in the right place at the right time. However, essential chance here operates in a context in which forces making for regularity are also present. Individuals pursue their diverse ends, often in situations of great uncertainty, but in an informed way guided by a common rationality and under various in part shared normative and non-normative constraints. What might then appear at first sight as essential chance at work can often be shown to be at least in some degree socially conditioned.

For example, in early work, Jencks (1972) emphasised the role of 'sheer luck' in relative success or failure in economic life; but, as he himself came later to accept (Jencks, 1979), individuals' experience of such luck, whether good or bad, can be significantly influenced by their social milieux. And as Granovetter's work has served to show, the occurrence of one kind of luck cited by Jencks – 'chance acquaintances who steer you to one line of work rather than another' – is very likely to be conditioned by features of individuals' social networks, so that it is possible to 'pursue a systematic analysis of this variety of "luck" by placing it in a social structural context' (Granovetter, 1995: xi).

Thus, in analyses made at the population level – that is, covering relatively large numbers of individuals – probabilistic regularities in

[2] As a biologist, Monod's main concern was to establish the essentially chance element in evolution. The processes through which mutations in DNA sequences occur, he sought to show, have no connection with – are quite independent of – the effects that follow from the modified protein, the interactions it ensures, the reactions it catalyses and so on. At King's College, Cambridge during the 1960s, I benefited greatly from several conversations with Jacques Monod on 'chance and necessity' in biology and in social life.

social life of many kinds do still emerge despite the pervasiveness of essential chance – though often they are regularities of a complex and not readily visible, let alone transparent, kind. And it is then these regularities that, under the auspices of operational chance, can be treated as the explananda for which sociological explanations may properly be sought.

In contrast, with distinctive, singular events, essential chance tends to take on a far more dominant role and to operate in a way that is far less easily 'tamable'. Although it may be possible, at least after the fact, to suggest certain prevailing regularities and perhaps underlying causal mechanisms that could have been conducive to such events, in their actual occurrence the – inherently improbable – intersection of preceding events tends to be involved, and often quite crucially so. It is this fact that appears to be overlooked by those who urge that sociologists should seek to explain singular events or singular complexes of events, such as – to take examples from Mahoney and Goertz (2006: 230) – the outbreak of the two world wars or the collapse of the Soviet Union. In arguing thus, these authors claim that natural scientists are very ready to apply their theories to account for 'particular outcomes', and they give as an example the explanation provided by the physicist Richard Feynman for the NASA shuttle *Challenger* disaster of January 1986. However, this example actually serves rather well to bring out the weakness of the position that Mahoney and Goertz take up.

The immediate cause of the disaster at the launch of *Challenger* was the failure of the rubber seals on a solid rocket booster joint, through their loss of resilience at low temperatures. And the physics of this failure were indeed dramatically demonstrated by Feynman. At a session of the Presidential Commission of Inquiry into the disaster, he soaked a sample of the rubber used for the seals in a glass of iced water on his desk – and then snapped it. But the problem of the resilience of the seals was in fact well-known, and what was crucial was that during a teleconference the night before the launch, confusion occurred over the relationship that existed between air temperature and the probability of the seals losing their effectiveness. The statistical data hurriedly considered came only from previous launches in which some damage to the seals had actually occurred, and analyses of these data did not strongly indicate that, with the temperature that was forecast for the morning, the launch should be postponed – whereas what subsequently emerged was that *if data from all launches had been examined*, the results would have far more clearly shown that a major risk existed (Dalal, Fowlkes and Hoadley, 1989). After much argument, the launch was allowed to go ahead and the seals failed.

The key point to note here is that while sociological theory could perhaps, as claimed by Vaughan (1996), be of help in explaining prevailing contextual features that made it more likely that a shuttle disaster of some kind *might* happen – for example, NASA's organisational culture and its 'normalisation of deviance' in regard to safety issues – it could scarcely lead to an explanation for the fact that this particular disaster *did* happen. As Popper (1957: 116–17, 143–7) has maintained, with due acknowledgement to Max Weber (1906/1949), when, in order to explain some 'actual, singular, or specific event', several different causal processes have to be invoked, with different theoretical groundings, the explanation that results *will not itself be a theoretical one*. It will be an explanation of a quite different kind: that is, a *historical* explanation, which involves an account of the unfolding of all relevant prior events, including their quite contingent intersections and their consequences – essential chance at work – up to the point at which the event of interest was actually brought about. In short, what is involved is a narrative of a highly specific, place- and time-linked kind, and one that is necessarily given *ex post*.[3]

---

[3] In her book on the *Challenger* launch decision, Vaughan (1996: xiii) claims that she provides 'a sociological explanation' of this decision, but also, on the same page, that she provides 'a historical ethnography' of the sequence of events that led up to it. The latter claim is more compelling than the former. Vaughan's detailed account of this sequence of events (see ch. 8 especially) does in fact serve well to show how, at a number of different points, essential chance came crucially into play.

It may be noted that Mahoney has more recently associated himself with the view that historical explanations are indeed distinctive in being concerned with the causes of particular past occurrences, and that 'the question of whether and how the resulting explanation might then be generalised is a secondary concern' (Mahoney, Kimball and Koivu, 2009: 116). But, very strangely, this is in a paper devoted to the logic of historical explanation *in the social sciences* – in which, one might suppose, the search for theoretically grounded explanations than can extend beyond particular cases must be a *primary* concern.

Fortunately, despite the misguided encouragement that some would offer, social scientists do not all that often attempt to explain singular events, and thus the main importance of the foregoing argument actually arises in another case: that is, where sociologists seek to explain events or complexes of events that are grouped together under some rubric *as if* they were characterised by significant regularities, but where no compelling demonstration of this has been provided. For purposes of illustration of the difficulties that arise, I will take what is claimed to be the sociology of revolutions, although I could have equally well taken, say, the supposed sociology of economic crises or of various historical trajectories, such as, say, 'routes' to authoritarianism or democracy or 'paths' to modernisation.

In a review article, Goldstone (2003: 50, see also 1995) has maintained that 'steady progress' has been achieved in the sociology of revolutions. This progress has resulted from the application of essentially inductive procedures to detailed case studies of 'finite sets' of revolutions, rather than from the analysis of samples of revolutions taken from some 'pre-defined universe'. As studies of particular revolutions have accumulated, Goldstone claims, knowledge of the different causal processes that may be involved has grown, allowing wider-ranging and more secure generalisations about the occurrence of revolutions to be made, and, indeed, creating the possibility of their prediction. Goldstone (1995: 45) himself has sought to integrate this body of work into what he terms a 'conjunctural process model' of revolutions. This proposes that a society 'is careening [sic] toward revolution' when three conditions apply: (i) the state loses effectiveness in its ability to command resources and obedience; (ii) elites are alienated from the state and in heightened conflict over the distribution of power and status; and (iii) a large or strategic proportion of the population can be readily mobilised for protest actions.

As Tilly (1995: 139–40) has observed, these conditions are in themselves so close to *defining* an actual revolutionary situation as to make Goldstone's model of limited potential in explaining how revolutions come about. But what may further be objected is that what is empirically claimed does not even amount to a number of established regularities in the social processes leading up to revolutions that could constitute appropriate sociological explananda. For, as Goldstone appears to accept, his 'conjunctural' conditions for revolution *have no inherent tendency to come together*; whether or not they do so in particular cases has to be regarded as quite contingent. And he does indeed explicitly acknowledge that his model 'says nothing' about the causes of societies moving towards a revolutionary situation, and suggests that no fixed set of such causes exists (Goldstone, 1995: 45).

It is therefore difficult to see that any compelling argument is made out for the viability of a sociology of revolutions. If induction from successive case studies does not lead to the establishment of empirical regularities in the pre-conditions for revolutions, in their outbreak, in their development, in the factors associated with their success or failure and so on, but instead reveals ever-widening variation from case to case, then the possibility of some *theoretical* explanation of revolutions in terms of the systematic processes that are at work is clearly undermined.[4] And what, one may argue, is in turn indicated is that major weight must be given to factors that are specific

---

[4] I should stress here that although, as indicated later in the chapter, I have serious doubts about the methodology that Goldstone favours – that is, relying on induction from 'finite sets' of cases – I do not believe that this methodology is itself the source of the failure to establish empirical regularities in relation to revolutions. I would entirely agree with Goldstone (2003: 43) that large-N, sample-based studies of revolutions have 'not been terribly fruitful' and have in fact done no better in this regard.

to individual cases, including their interaction through the operation of essential chance. In other words, what would appear appropriate is not a sociology of revolutions but, at most, a comparative history, which, following Popper, would have to be recognised as an intellectual undertaking of a quite different kind. That is to say, one in which explanations advanced for different revolutions are compared, with due account being taken of the particular concatenations of events involved, and with a concern as much for the diversity of possible revolutionary processes as for common features.[5]

It is in this regard of interest to find that among professional historians studying revolutions, the tendency has in fact increasingly been to downplay regularities that might be supposed to exist across cases and to emphasise their individual distinctiveness. For example, the author of the most comprehensive study to date of 'the English Revolution' of the seventeenth century remarks in his concluding chapter that 'I am sceptical about the quest for a morphology of revolution that will accommodate the upheavals that began in France in 1789, in Russia in 1917, in China under Chairman Mao, and other later convulsions elsewhere' (Woolrych, 2002: 792).[6]

The position that I have taken up in the foregoing might be regarded as unduly negative: that is, as seeking to impose unnecessary limits on sociological ambition. But those who are inclined to such a view might wish to reflect on the fact that there is no reason to suppose that the range of sociological explanation is infinite – no

---

[5] Goldstone and others seeking to create a sociology of revolutions do sometimes alternatively describe their objective as that of providing a 'comparative historical analysis' of revolutions – but without any evident recognition of the differences that arise.

[6] See also the observations of the pioneering revisionist historian of the French Revolution, Alfred Cobban (1965: esp. chs 1–3), whom I was fortunate enough to have as a teacher. His work in particular serves to underline the point that scepticism of the kind that Woolrych expresses in no way precludes historians of revolutions from making use of sociological concepts, or indeed of sociological theory, that have been developed in other areas. But the distinction between historical and sociological explanation remains. Anyone doubtful of it, and thus inclined to follow Mahoney and Goertz in believing in the possibility of a sociological explanation of the outbreak of the First World War, would do well to read Clark's (2013) superb historical account, or at least pp. 361–4 and the Conclusion.

reason to suppose that there can be a sociology of anything and everything – and that it is therefore important to have some idea of where,
and on what grounds, the *boundaries* of sociological explanation are
to be drawn. It is moreover relevant to note that excessive ambition
has its costs. Thus, after the events of 1989–90, sociologists did in fact
have to face much criticism for their failure to anticipate the collapse
of the Soviet Union – criticism that could have been avoided, or at
least effectively rejected, if within the discipline a clearer awareness
and more explicit recognition had been present of where a historical
rather than a sociological explanation is called for. If this had been the
case, then, as Hechter (1995: 1523) has observed, sociologists would
have had no need 'to hang their heads in shame'. As for Goldstone's
(1995) claim that, in the light of his model, he would in fact have
been able predict the revolutions associated with the Soviet collapse,
Runciman's (1998: 16) comment is brutal but to the point: 'So maybe
you could, Jack. And if you could, you should. But you didn't.'[7]

As a coda to this chapter, some remarks may be apposite on the
use of *logical* rather than statistical methods in sociological analysis,
since the difficulties that arise in the application of logical methods
serve to bring out in another way the dangers of pursuing sociological
explanations where it is historical explanations that are required. It
was in fact with Skocpol's (1979) early study of revolutions – specifically, with her use of John Stuart Mill's (1843/1973–74) 'method of
agreement' and 'method of difference' – that logical methods came
into prominence in sociology; and while Goldstone would appear to
apply such methods in only an informal manner, others who would
share in his commitment to working inductively from case studies
have sought to develop them beyond Mill. Most notably, Charles
Ragin (1987) has proposed the use of set theory and Boolean algebra in

---

[7] Economists have of course come under criticism for their failure to predict the
financial crash of 2008, and it is notable that some at least of their number have
taken the view that such prediction lies beyond the scope of economics as a social
science, not least on account of the part likely to be played in events of the kind in
question by historical specificities.

what has become known as 'qualitative comparative analysis' (QCA), and it is on this method that I focus.

QCA aims at showing the conditions under which a certain outcome does or does not occur, with the various conditions considered being themselves also treated as binary: in effect, as present or absent. On the basis of case studies, a 'truth table' is constructed, showing which sets of conditions are associated with the outcome occurring or not occurring, and Boolean algebra is then used in order to collapse the truth table into a minimal formula. In the strong version of QCA, this Boolean equation is taken as a 'causal recipe' that gives all of the combinations of conditions that are necessary and/or sufficient for the outcome in question to be realised. In a weaker version, which of late appears more often to be advanced – if with a good deal of equivocation (see e.g. Rihoux and Marx, 2013: 168–9) – the Boolean equation is represented as simply a means of summarising results from a number of case studies in a form that invites, or, at most, could suggest, causal explanations. In this weaker version, QCA might then appear as a possible way of establishing empirical regularities in regard to some social phenomenon that would in turn constitute sociological explananda of a legitimate kind.

However, whether QCA is understood as a source of causal recipes or as an essentially descriptive method, it is open to serious objections on grounds that have been most cogently expressed by Lieberson (2004) and by Lucas and Szatrowski (2014). What these authors are concerned to stress is that QCA as a method of logical rather than statistical analysis must assume a quite deterministic rather than a probabilistic social world.[8] That is to say, it can make

---

[8] In a later work, Ragin (2000) has moved beyond his original formulation of QCA in proposing that in place of 'crisp' sets, implying strictly binary categorisations, 'fuzzy' sets may be used. This new approach entails a significant shift away from logical and towards statistical analysis, in that it involves measurement, albeit rather crude and often arbitrary, of the degree to which cases belong to particular sets; and it can also be used to implement a probabilistic rather than a deterministic understanding of causation, although at cost of such oxymorons as 'almost necessary' and 'nearly sufficient'. I do not therefore consider fuzzy-set QCA in the context of the present

no allowance for the operation of essential chance in this world, nor, moreover, for chance simply in the form of error in our – supposed – knowledge about it (see further Goldthorpe, 2007: vol. 1, ch. 3; Hug, 2013). In turn, therefore, QCA can take no account of the extent to which a truth table derived from case studies may contain results that are in effect *random*: that is, in consequence of the social world not in fact being deterministic or in consequence just of data error. And for this reason, Boolean summary equations can then easily lead, as Lieberson (2004) argues, to 'massive over-interpretation', or, as Lucas and Szatrowski (2014) would claim, to causal explanations that are simply mistaken.[9] Another way of putting the point here being made would be to say that QCA may often be incapable of distinguishing signal from noise. And Lieberson has indeed demonstrated the possibility that QCA could well produce Boolean equations from truth tables that were *entirely noise*: that is, that were generated by entirely random processes.

In response to this, it has been argued (e.g. Ragin and Rihoux, 2004) that such random truth tables would in fact be readily shown up as such, in that they would contain many contradictions – that is, instances of identical sets of conditions being associated with the

discussion of difficulties associated with purely logical analysis. However, as shown by Krogslund, Choi and Poertner (2015), the results of fuzzy-set QCA are highly sensitive to quite small changes in the parameters applied in the 'calibration' of set membership and in then carrying out the Boolean minimisation. And the question does thus arise of what fuzzy-set QCA can do that cannot be done more simply and reliably through existing statistical methods such as, say, loglinear modelling or latent class analysis (on which, see further Chapter 7). As Achen (2005: 29) has commented, Ragin's repeated assertion that quantitative methods of data analysis in the social sciences are restricted to regression analyses estimating context-free net effects is 'a mystifying claim indeed'.

[9] Interestingly, Lucas and Szatrowski (2014) seek to illustrate their case by showing that a QCA analysis of the – immediate – cause of the *Challenger* disaster, previously discussed in this chapter, gives an explanation that is in contradiction with that generally accepted by engineers and also by the Presidential Commission of Inquiry: that is, that the disaster was precipitated simply by the failure at low temperatures of the rubber seals on the rocket booster. The QCA analysis would imply that an interaction with other factors was also necessary to the failure – despite there being no independent evidence of this.

outcome of interest both occurring and not occurring – and that it is a standard task in QCA to resolve such contradictions, usually by introducing new conditions, before proceeding further. But this response turns out to be inadequate. On the basis of simulations, Marx (2010) has shown that contradictions do not necessarily arise with randomly generated truth tables. What is crucial is the number of cases covered and the number of conditions involved. More specifically, Marx's (2010: 155) results lead him to suggest that '[QCA] applications with more than 7 conditions (including the outcome) and applications where the proportion of conditions on cases is higher than .33 are not able to distinguish real from random data'. And his overview of studies using QCA (Marx, 2010: Table 4) then reveals that a substantial proportion were in fact of this very questionable kind.

At the root of the problem that arises here is the fact that, as a logical method assuming a deterministic world, QCA must aim to account *fully* for all cases considered. In statistical language, it must aim to account for 100% of the variance in the outcome of interest. This means, as Seawright (2005: 16–18) has pointed out, that in QCA *all* conditions that are causally relevant to the outcome of interest in the population of cases studied have to be included: not only those that operate with some regularity across cases, but also quite 'idiosyncratic' – and, one might suspect, purely chance – conditions that may be of relevance only in this or that particular instance. Thus, it is always likely that the number of conditions that will need to be considered and their ratio to the number of cases will be pushed up towards the danger levels that Marx identifies, and that would seem in practice to be frequently exceeded.[10]

---

[10] Even where QCA is applied to data-sets with quite large Ns (see e.g. Cooper, 2005), the problem of over-interpretation may still arise in that Boolean equations can be arrived at that imply complex interaction effects which, if incorporated into, say, a loglinear model, would not prove statistically significant or, in other words, could easily reflect merely chance aspects of the data (see Krogslund, Choi and Poertner, 2015: 50–1).

Marx (2010: 147) himself aptly characterises the problem as one of 'uniqueness'. As the number of conditions distinguished approximates the number of cases analysed, the point is being reached at which each case has to be seen as representing a unique configuration of conditions: that is, there are *no* regularities. At this point, the possibility of contradictions is eliminated but the Boolean equation produced becomes meaningless, in that it could apply as well to random data as to those actually derived from the cases under study. An alternative way of putting the matter, to revert to the earlier discussion of this chapter, would be as follows. Where a situation of the kind in question arises, what is being indicated is that – as in the case of the supposed sociology of revolutions – an attempt is being made to provide a sociological explanation for events that are not in fact characterised by sufficient regularity to allow for this, nor indeed for a theoretical explanation of any kind. Or, in other words, to the extent that the problem of uniqueness threatens in the case of events or complexes of events, it is historical rather than sociological explanation that is called for.

Insofar as proponents of QCA propose a solution to this problem, it would appear to be that of limiting explanatory analyses to populations of cases that are deemed to be 'comparable' in the sense of being 'causally homogeneous' or, in other words, in allowing a contradiction-free truth table to be obtained with a relatively small number of conditions. But to resort thus to 'constructed' populations (Ragin, 2013: 173; and see Goertz and Mahoney, 2009) rather than ones that are defined independently of the explanatory model to be put forward – and, presumably, in the light of the analyst's prior substantive interests – must mean that the scope conditions of the model are set in a quite arbitrary way. The description of population regularities and their explanation are confounded; and only those cases are to be considered where a particular explanatory model can be shown to fit. While all theories in the social sciences are likely to require scope conditions of some kind, the appropriate procedure (see further Chapter 9) must be to develop theories in order to account for quite independently established explananda and then to discover, through further research, how adequate to the task these theories are and what their limitations, including their scope conditions, might be. Otherwise, one has from the start explanatory models that, like an ill-cut suit, just fit where they touch.

Examination of the difficulties faced by logical methods of analysis, based on the assumption of a deterministic social world, does then help to highlight distinctive features of sociology understood as a population science based on the assumption of a probabilistic social world, and thus reliant on statistical methods. In this latter case, two limiting conditions are recognised at the outset. First, it is accepted, on the grounds set out in this chapter, that appropriate explananda for sociology will be only events of a kind that can be shown empirically to be expressed in aggregate-level, probabilistic regularities, emergent from the states and behaviour of individual members of populations. And second, as will be discussed at greater length in the chapters that follow, it is accepted that variance in the outcomes of interest will be accounted for not totally, but only to the extent that this variance results from factors that can be regarded as operating in a systematic rather than an idiosyncratic or quite random manner (see King, Keohane and Verba, 1994: ch. 2 esp.).

5   Statistics, concepts and the objects of sociological study

Statistics has to be regarded as foundational for sociology as a population science in the sense that, as the means through which population regularities are established, it actually constitutes the explananda or 'objects of study' of sociology – although always in conjunction with the concepts that sociologists form.

In a population science, whatever its substantive concerns, statistical methods will be required in the primary task of establishing the extent and form of population regularities. In sociology understood as a population science, statistics does indeed contribute crucially in this way in regard to both data collection and data analysis – as I will argue at some length in Chapters 6 and 7. It is, however, important that prior consideration should be given to a further and deeper sense in which statistics is foundational for sociology.

In this connection, a paper by a leading historian of statistics, Stephen Stigler (1999: ch. 10), provides key insights. Stigler seeks to bring out the significant differences that exist between the part that has come to be played by statistical methods in the social sciences and the uses to which such methods had previously been put in various natural sciences.

Stigler begins by noting that statistical methods were quite widely drawn on in astronomy from the eighteenth century onwards. This was, however, for a very specific purpose: namely, that of handling observational error. In studying the positions and movements of celestial bodies, astronomers believed that they had a correct theory to guide them – the Newtonian theory – and the prime purpose of the observations they made was to allow them to quantify this theory in its particular applications. For example, given that Jupiter travelled around the sun in an ellipse, what they wished to know were the coefficients of the equation for that ellipse. In pursuing work of this kind, astronomers did, however, face the difficulty that different observers, or perhaps the same observer on different occasions, produced different results: that is to say, astronomical observations were subject to error. Statistical methods were then seen as the solution – as the means, in effect, of separating truth from error. True values were out there to be obtained, and by exploiting such devices as the Gaussian 'error curve' – or normal distribution – and the method of least squares, a precursor of regression, error-prone observations could be processed so as to reach the best possible estimates of these true values: that is, by taking the mean of the distribution or the line of least squares.

From the mid-nineteenth century, Stigler further observes, early behavioural scientists, such as Fechner, Ebbinghaus and Peirce, also began to apply statistical methods, notably in 'psychophysical' studies of such phenomena as sensitivity, reaction times and memory. In this case, the purpose was not to deal with problems of observational error directly but rather to try to protect against erroneous inferences from observations through the appropriate design of experiments. In particular, techniques of randomisation were used in order to create a 'baseline' against which experimental effects, achieved under systematically varied conditions, could be reliably assessed.[1] Statistically informed experimental design, Stigler (1999: 193) suggests, provided 'a novel surrogate for the anchor of Newtonian law' that was enjoyed by the astronomers. And again, as with the astronomers, the underlying assumption was that a quite independent reality was being studied, with statistics being simply the means of acquiring a better knowledge of that reality.

However, what Stigler is then concerned to show is that as, from the later nineteenth century, statistical methods came increasingly to be used in the social sciences, a quite new and more complex situation

---

[1] Stigler remarks that the introduction of randomised experiments is usually associated with Fisher, but adds that Peirce at least 'was clear on what he was doing and why, and his "what and why" were the same as Fisher's' (Stigler, 1999: 193–4).

emerged. For social scientists, lacking any equivalent of Newtonian theory or, for the most part, opportunities for experimental research, statistical methods took on a significantly different and indeed significantly larger role. They served not merely as a means of obtaining less error-prone, more reliable knowledge of independently existing objects of study but rather *as a means in themselves of creating such objects of study.*

The contrast begins to emerge with the work of Quetelet (1835/1842, 1846, 1869) previously cited. While for astronomers the normal distribution simply expressed the distribution of errors around the true values that they sought, for Quetelet, and for his followers in the founding of quantitative sociology, the normal distribution was of *substantive* interest. If it could be established in relation to population rates of marriage, illegitimacy, suicide, crime and the like, it could then be taken as defining, through its centre, probabilistic attributes of *l'homme moyen*, or indeed of *l'homme type* of the particular society in question (see further Goldthorpe, 2007: vol. 2, ch. 8).[2] As noted in Chapter 1, Quetelet did later move on from such simple typological thinking to recognise the reality and importance of what might be called subpopulation variation. It was, however, only with the work of Galton (1889a) and his successors that the statistics of variation decisively superseded that of averages – leading to the development of modern methods of the multivariate analysis of individual-level data.[3] And it was only with this completion of the

---

[2] An attempt at clarifying the situation came in an important paper by Edgeworth, in which he distinguished between 'observations', the mean of which is real, and 'statistics', the mean of which is 'fictitious' or, that is, a construct of the investigator. Thus, '...observations are copies of one original; statistics are different originals affording one "generic portrait"' (Edgeworth, 1885: 139–40). The statistics to which Edgeworth referred in illustrating his argument were economic statistics – those of prices, exports and imports – as well as 'moral statistics' of the kind on which Quetelet focused.

[3] Durkheim (1897/1952) has often been regarded as the great pioneer of multivariate analysis in sociology in his study of suicide. However, while Durkheim went beyond Quetelet in the range of factors he considered in relation to variance in rates of suicide in national populations and their subpopulations, and also in his attempts at

transition from typological to population thinking (see Mayr, 1982: 47) that it became fully apparent that the role played by statistics in the social sciences was 'fundamentally different from its role in much of physical science' (Stigler, 1999: 199). The results obtained by fitting a statistical model to the observational data – in other words, the probabilistic regularities thus displayed – *constituted in themselves what existed to be further analysed and explained.*

If, then, statistics are to be seen as in this way foundational for the social sciences in a deeper sense than is often appreciated – that is, as actually creating their objects of study – questions are likely to arise over what might be called the ontological status of these objects. What 'reality' can they claim to express? Stigler (1999: 199) would himself regard them as being 'no less real' than the objects of study of physical science. And support for this position can be derived from a perceptive paper by Louçã (2008). In arguing for statistics as 'the *motum* for the modern revolution in science', Louçã (2008: 3) observes that statistics developed historically under two different assumptions. Initially, statistics supposed error to be entirely an attribute of the observer; but subsequently, and far more consequentially, it supposed 'error' – in the sense of variation with some degree of randomness – to be itself an inherent attribute of reality, social *or* natural. *Statistics, then, provides the access to such a reality.* And Louçã goes on to argue – diverging somewhat from Stigler in this respect – that it was actually a natural science, evolutionary biology, that was the first 'to be reconstructed on probabilistic foundations', although taking over models from statistical physics (see the discussion of Chapter 1).

However, while argument on these lines is in itself compelling, and obviously sits well with the claim I have made that it is empirically established probabilistic regularities that are the proper

explaining this variance, he had little understanding of the 'new English statistics' as pioneered by Galton. His analyses were not of a probabilistic but rather of a logical and deterministic kind, following in effect Mill's canon of 'concomitant variation'. Thus, Durkheim had no clear understanding of the concept of partial as opposed to perfect correlation (see further Goldthorpe, 2007: vol. 2, 201–3).

explananda of sociology understood as a population science, a further issue has still to be addressed. If it is the case that, for sociology thus understood, statistics is foundational in serving to constitute its objects of study, it has to be recognised that statistical methods cannot fulfil this role unaided. They can do so only in conjunction with the *concepts* that sociologists create and that are then made operational in the variables that are included in statistical analyses. And, for this reason, questions of the ontological status of such regularities as might be demonstrated by these analyses could be thought to resurface.

In the natural sciences, it has been supposed – although with some dissension (see, for a review, Bird and Tobin, 2012 and later in this chapter) – that at least certain basic conceptual schemata can be taken as referring to 'natural kinds', or, that is, can be understood as distinguishing between entities that are already clearly separated in nature itself. The classifications of fundamental physical particles or of chemical elements would be obvious examples. But, whatever the strength of the case for believing that conceptually the natural world can be 'carved at its joints' – to use Plato's expression[4] – few would regard this as being possible with the social world. The concepts applied in the social sciences, rather than being directly 'given' by the way the social world actually is, would be generally accepted as the products of human efforts to grapple cognitively with this world, so that quite different, and perhaps competing and conflicting, *découpages conceptuels* may be adopted.

For present purposes, the crucial question that then arises is the following: Are the regularities that sociology as a population science would aim to establish as its basic explananda, in resulting from statistical analyses informed by some particular conceptual approach, constructions of no more than an arbitrary kind? Are they, in other

---

[4] *Phaedrus* 265d–6a. Plato compares the task of defining both natural and also moral qualities with that of a butcher cutting meat. This is best done if the cuts follow the joints that are already there.

words, the result simply of applying one among a wide variety of other possible conceptual approaches, and, moreover, approaches that may well be 'incommensurable' and thus allow for no assessment of their relative adequacy in representing social reality? Extreme 'constructivists', such as those associated with the so-called 'post-Mertonian' sociology of science, would indeed claim that this is the case. They would argue that no entities – not even in the natural world – can be supposed to exist independently of the way in which they are conceptually formed, and that consequently, as Woolgar (1988: 73) has put it, 'there is no object beyond discourse'. However, there would seem little reason to accept such a position – and much to be said for rejecting it, whether in regard to the social or the natural sciences.[5]

As Popper (1994: ch. 2 esp.) has argued in seeking to expose 'the myth of the framework', different conceptual approaches need not be incommensurable; often, in fact, they do, at least to some extent, 'translate' one into another. For example, Copernicus could show how all astronomical observations that could be fitted into a geocentric system could, through a simple translation method, be fitted into a heliocentric system. Moreover, to the extent that translation between different approaches is not possible, rational procedures still exist for making comparative evaluations of them. In particular, one may consider, first, the extent to which different concepts can be effectively

---

[5] Many sociologists who are attracted by extreme constructivist views, perhaps because of their seeming 'radicalism', would appear not to realise their full implications (see Hacking, 2000: ch. 3). What must follow is that a body of existing scientific knowledge – for example, present-day physics – has to be seen as being of a quite *contingent* character, rather than being in any way determined by the way the world actually is. Thus, under, say, different sociocultural circumstances to those that prevailed in the past, an alternative, non-equivalent but no less 'successful' physics to that we have today could have developed. The big difficulty that arises with this position is that no one has ever been able to give any idea at all of what this alternative physics might have looked like. As an amusing *reductio ad absurdum* of extreme constructivism – presumably unintended – one may note the questioning by Latour (2000) of the conclusion reached by archaeologists examining the mummy of Ramses II that he died, *c.* 1213 BC, of tuberculosis. Given that the tuberculosis bacillus was only discovered – that is, constructed – by Robert Koch in 1882, Latour asks if this conclusion is not as 'anachronistic' as claiming that Ramses' death was caused by a Marxist upheaval, a machine gun or a Wall Street crash.

applied in research and, second, the extent to which, when so applied, they are *revealing* in regard to phenomena of substantive interest.

So far as the applicability of concepts in research is concerned, the key consideration is that of how far they can be expressed through measurement instruments – classifications, scales and so on – that have an adequate degree of reliability and validity (with reference to the human and social sciences, see e.g. Carmines and Zeller, 1979; Bohrnstedt, 2010). 'Reliability' refers to the degree to which an instrument by means of which a concept is made operational as a variable can be consistently applied, so that, for example, it gives the same results under conditions where it should in fact do so. Various tests of reliability are well established. 'Validity' is a more complex idea and different forms can be distinguished. But that most important – usually labelled as 'construct' validity – refers to the degree to which an instrument can be shown empirically to capture what, conceptually, it is supposed to capture.[6] What has then to be stressed is that arguments over the merits of one concept, or conceptual scheme, as opposed to another can have little point without being grounded in evidence about the possibility of their being reliably and validly applied in actual research procedures – but that such evidence, once produced, can then provide objective grounds for comparative evaluations.

Given concepts that have been made operational for research purposes with an adequate degree of reliability and validity, the

---

[6] Another form of validity – usually labelled as 'criterion' validity – concerns the degree to which, when an instrument translates a concept into a variable, this variable correlates with other variables with which, theoretically, it would be expected to correlate. Unfortunately, there would appear to be no standard terminology, and some authors in fact apply the labels of 'construct' and 'criterion' validity in the reverse way to that I have used. It may also be noted that the degree of attention paid to the validity of concepts appears to vary quite widely across the human and social sciences. It is perhaps most developed in psychology; but in economics, while concepts tend to be derived rather stringently from theory, questions of how validly they are then made operational in research seem relatively little addressed, even in the case of such basic concepts as 'employment' and 'unemployment', 'permanent income', 'skill' and 'human capital'. Sociology might be given an intermediate position but would undoubtedly benefit by moving closer to psychology.

question of how far they prove revealing in their application is, again, one that can be empirically addressed. In discussion of concepts in much of what passes as sociological theory, little reference is found to what is achieved when the concepts in question are actually put to work in specific cases. But it is a frequent feature of at least quantitative research in sociology that attempts are made to show that much the same results are produced with different conceptual approaches in some area of interest (in other words, that these approaches *are* translatable), or that different approaches have advantages and disadvantages in different respects, or that one approach is in general more revealing than others.

To provide illustration of the foregoing, one could take the case of the conceptualisation of social stratification. Up to the middle of the last century, much discussion centred on the usefulness of Marxist class analysis in the context of emerging 'managerial capitalism' and the growth of 'intermediate strata' – although this discussion proceeded with only a rather loose articulation with empirical studies (see e.g. Dahrendorf, 1959). But then, chiefly in the US, attempts were made to provide means of treating social stratification more systematically, in particular in relatively large-scale survey research, through the use of scales aimed at capturing concepts of occupational prestige or of occupational 'socioeconomic status' based on levels of education and income (Duncan, 1961; Treiman, 1977). Scales of this kind are still produced and used, but now less widely than before; and from the later twentieth century, a movement can be traced back to the use of class concepts, although now of varying kinds: for example, ones represented as being of Weberian and Durkheimian, as well as of Marxist inspiration (Wright, 2005). And a still more recent shift has been towards a multidimensional approach, involving distinctions between class and status as qualitatively different forms of stratification, and further between these 'relational' aspects of stratification, on the one hand, and 'attributional' aspects, such as income and wealth or education, on the other (Chan and Goldthorpe, 2007; Goldthorpe, 2012).

In the course of these developments, much argument, and indeed often sharp controversy, has occurred among those taking up different conceptual positions. Yet it is still possible to discern progress. For example, occupational prestige and socioeconomic status scales did lead to advances in regard to reliability, and although such scales have proved vulnerable to criticism on grounds of validity (e.g. Hauser and Warren, 1997) – that is, concerning what exactly it is that they are intended to measure and how well they do it – a greater awareness of the importance of validity has thus been created. This has then been reflected in the case of the new class schemata that have been advanced. Especially where a schema has been considered or actually taken over for use in official statistics, extensive testing of its construct validity has been involved (see e.g. in the case of the British National Statistics Socio-Economic Classification and a proposed European extension of this classification, Rose and Pevalin, 2003; Rose, Pevalin and O'Reilly, 2005; Rose and Harrison, 2010).

Moreover, argument over the merits of different conceptual approaches to social stratification, as outlined in the previous paragraph, has increasingly been conducted not *in abstracto* but rather in terms of what they do or do not show up in their particular applications and of their consequent advantages and disadvantages – as, for example, in the analysis of social mobility (Marshall et al., 1988: ch. 4; Jonsson et al., 2009; Erikson, Goldthorpe and Hällsten, 2012), or again of social inequalities in such areas as health, educational attainment and cultural participation (Jaeger, 2007; Torssander and Erikson, 2009, 2010; Chan, 2010; Buis, 2013; Bukodi and Goldthorpe, 2013; Bukodi, Erikson and Goldthorpe, 2014). In other words, attention has come to centre on the relationship between concepts and the social reality that they are intended to illuminate *as this can be demonstrated through empirical research*. And what is then made apparent is that this relationship is not arbitrary but rather one of *interdependence*. While sociologists are free to choose between different conceptual approaches, social reality can, as it were, strike back, in that, once put into use, particular choices will carry empirical implications that can then be compared, to better or worse effect, with those that follow from other approaches.

Finally in this connection, it may be questioned how far any sharp discontinuities in processes of concept formation and application do in fact arise between the social and the natural sciences. Consider, for example, the concept of species, which is of course fundamental in biology. In the Linnean era, species were generally taken as referring to natural kinds: that is, to entities existing quite independently of human observation. But in the post-Darwinian era, with the recognition of evolution, the idea of species as natural kinds was found increasingly problematic, and by the present time, a whole range of 'species concepts' has emerged. These entail not only different understandings of the numbers of species and of appropriate criteria for allocating organisms to species but, further, more basic divergences of view – quite comparable to those that arise in debates on conceptualisation in sociology – over the sense, if any, in which species might be regarded as having an objective reality rather than being no more than researchers' constructs (see e.g. Pavlinov, 2013).

At the same time, though, a further similarity can be noted. Despite what has become known as 'the species problem', biologists appear still to be able to get on with productive research, and to do so in much the same way as, I have suggested, could be taken to represent best practice among sociologists: that is, by avoiding either extreme 'realist' or extreme 'nominalist' positions[7] and by adhering, at all events *de facto*, to what might be called an empirically disciplined conceptual pluralism. This means accepting that, in concept formation, researchers do play an active cognitive role rather than simply recognising some inherent structure of the reality of interest to them, and that differing research interests or theoretical orientations may therefore lead to the adoption of different conceptual positions.

---

[7] Biologists, being perhaps better read than sociologists in the history of philosophy, tend to discuss fundamental issues of conceptualisation in terms of realism and nominalism rather than of 'social construction', but it is essentially the same issues that are involved (Hacking, 2000: ch. 3).

But it also means accepting that a reality does exist independently of researchers' cognitive efforts, that this will influence the results they obtain from the application of the concepts they favour and that it is then in terms of these results that the value of these concepts will ultimately have to be judged.[8]

In sum, the probabilistic regularities that statistical methods serve to establish as the objects of study of sociology as a population science – or, as, I would wish to say, as its basic explananda – *are* constructed. Indeed, one could say that they are doubly constructed: first, through the concepts that sociologists make operational as variables in statistical analyses, and second, through the form that these analyses take. However, these regularities are not constructions of an arbitrary kind because quite detached from any social reality. This reality is not only supposed but is actually *expressed* – actually makes itself felt – through the results that are then achieved from the analyses undertaken: that is, in whether or not any regularities are in fact shown up, and, if so, with what strength, in what form, with what extension over place and time and so on. With different conceptual approaches and kinds of statistical analysis, different versions of this reality are likely to be represented. For example, a study of social mobility based on scales of socioeconomic status and causal path analysis will produce a different account, for the same society at the same time, to that produced by a study based on a categorical class schema and loglinear modelling. But where, as is to be expected, differing accounts thus follow from differing conceptual and statistical

---

[8] One special problem in concept formation in the social sciences that has to be recognised is that of the 'double hermeneutic' (Giddens, 1984) or, as put more plainly by Hacking (2000: ch. 4), that of 'looping effects': that is, the problem that arises from the possibility that a concept, made operational, say, through a classification, may *interact with* social reality in that individuals respond to being thus classified in such a way that the reality is changed. Hacking discusses this problem in regard to the classification of mental disorders and deviance, but in such cases issues of what sociologists have for long understood as 'labelling' effects would appear to be handled without great difficulty. And Hacking's (2000: 108) claim that, in the social sciences, classifications are 'mostly interactive' would seem very wide of the mark (Goldthorpe, 2007: vol. 1, 6–7).

constructions, these accounts can be compared in order to see what each reveals or conceals, how far they are translatable into each other and, if seemingly contradictory results are produced, how these arise and what would be necessary for a resolution. And all of this can be regarded as part of normal scientific practice and progress.

6 Statistics and methods of data collection

In sociology as a population science, the foundational role played by statistics in establishing population regularities stems, in the first place, from the need for methods of data collection that are able to accommodate the degree of variability characteristic of human social life, in particular at the individual level, and that can thus provide an adequate basis for the analysis of regularities occurring within the variation that exists.

Over many decades now, the role of statistics in sociology has tended steadily to increase. Yet this tendency would seem to have attracted rather more in the way of criticism – for example, as expressing an unacceptable 'positivism' – than of attempts at explanation: that is, explanation of why it should be that two statistically informed methodologies, sample survey research and multivariate data analysis, should in fact, despite all opposition, have become so central to sociology.

As regards data collection, which is the concern of the present chapter, the following observation may be taken as a starting point. The editors of a leading text on social survey research, Wright and Marsden (2010: 4), make the scarcely disputable claim that 'the sample survey has emerged as the principal means of obtaining information on modern human populations', but they then have little, if anything, to say *about why this should be so*. What can, however, be shown, and has in the present context to be emphasised, is that the sample survey did not achieve its present prominence in some more or less fortuitous way. It did so because it represented the eventual solution to two (closely related) problems that persisted in social research from the mid-nineteenth through to the mid-twentieth century.

The first of these problems was that the data on human populations obtained from the censuses and registration procedures that were developed in Western societies from the later eighteenth century onwards, while for many purposes invaluable, had, if only on grounds of cost, to be quite restricted in their scope. Other methods of data collection were therefore needed through which population coverage could be traded off against the possibility of obtaining information of a wider-ranging yet also more detailed kind. However, the second problem then arose. If 'complete enumeration' was to be supplemented by such 'partial studies' – to use the language of the day – some appropriate methodology had to be developed for moving 'from part to whole' on a reliable basis.

An attempt at meeting the first problem came with the 'monographic' approach to social research, as advocated and practised most notably by Frédéric Le Play and his followers. Le Play proposed, and sought to implement, a methodology which entailed the first-hand and protracted study of individuals in the context of their families and communities – in effect, an early form of ethnographic case study (Zonabend, 1992). Information was to be collected on the economic conditions under which individuals lived, but in greater depth than in official statistics, together with information on their primary social relations, their life histories, their aspirations for the future, and their moral beliefs and values. Researchers needed to 'speak the same language' as the men and women they studied and to 'enter into their minds' (Silver, 1982: 41–75, 171–83).

Such research was thus designed – to use now modern terminology – to be intensive rather than extensive in its nature, with the emphasis being placed on the qualitative characteristics of the material obtained in each case, rather than on the number of cases studied. Thus, in the first edition of Le Play's own major work, he presented monographs relating to just thirty-six working-class families spread across different European countries; he extended this to fifty-seven families in the second edition (Le Play, 1877–79). A number of his followers produced similar collections, also dealing mainly with working-class living conditions and family relations.

However, while the Leplaysians introduced a way of collecting social data that could go beyond what was possible with complete enumeration, and that did indeed produce data of a kind hitherto lit-tle available – in particular, on family forms and family budgets – their approach ran into serious difficulties in dealing with the second problem previously noted: that of moving from part to whole. The Leplaysians clearly wished to take the findings of their monographs as a basis for advancing general propositions about European working classes; and, in order to justify this, the claim they made was that their cases were so selected as to be 'typical' – at least, say, of workers in particular occupations, industries or regions. But they then failed to provide any consistent or compelling account of how they actually achieved such selection for typicality. Le Play himself maintained that adequate guidance in this respect could be obtained from 'local authorities', such as civil servants, clergy or doctors, while some of his followers proposed that cases could be chosen that were shown by official statistics to be in various respects 'average' – making then an appeal to the Queteletian idea (see Chapters 1 and 5) that the average would represent the socially significant type, with variation around the average being merely contingent and thus of little scientific interest.

Such arguments, perhaps not surprisingly, met with a good deal of contemporary scepticism – extending in some instances to charges that the selection of cases was in fact biased so as to lend support to Le Play's socially conservative views.[1] And in the light of subsequent research, it has indeed become evident enough that generalisations of a quite mistaken kind were advanced – the most notable, perhaps, being that leading to what is now known by historical demographers as 'the myth of the extended family'. That is, Le Play's attempt to

---

[1] It was pointed out that where 'local authorities' guided the selection of cases, they might be expected to pick out families who were known to be supportive of the status quo rather than those who were in some way dissident; and suspicions of con-servative bias were only reinforced where the assumption was made that atypicality implied not only statistical but also social deviance. Several re-studies carried out in localities covered by Le Play's work did in fact claim to show less harmony in community and workplace relations and less satisfaction with the prevailing order than he had indicated (see Lazarsfeld, 1961; Silver, 1982: 54–75).

represent the extended family as being prevalent in pre-industrial Western as well as Eastern Europe (Laslett, 1972).

More importantly, though, as well as doubts being raised about the monographers' selection of cases, an objection to their approach of a yet more basic kind was made by a number of statisticians, even as they too recognised the need to move beyond complete enumeration in the collection of social data. A leading figure in this regard was Anders Kiaer, Director General of the Norwegian Bureau of Statistics from 1877 to 1913. What Kiaer (1895–96, 1903) and others argued was that, in designing partial studies, the monographers' quest for typicality, even if it could be realised, was still mistaken in principle. This was so because human populations had to be studied not in terms simply of social types but in such a way as to take account, as Kiaer put it (1895–96: 181), of 'all the variation of cases that one finds in life'. Thus, the aim in partial studies should not be to achieve typicality but rather to move from part to whole in a quite different way: that is, by selecting a *representative sample* of the population under investigation in the sense of one that would provide 'a true miniature of it' in respect of the full degree of variation existing among its members in all attributes of research interest.[2] In other words, what Kiaer was in effect urging was a shift from typological to population thinking in the methodology of data collection parallel to that which was occurring in the methodology of data analysis with the move from the Queteletian statistics of the average to the Galtonian statistics of variation.

Kiaer himself pioneered the method of what became known as 'purposive' (or sometimes as 'judgemental') sampling. With such sampling, census and other aggregate statistics were initially drawn on in order to select – in modern terminology – primary and secondary sampling units so that these would give an overall 'match' with the

---

[2] A strong echo of this argument is found in the study of working-class family budgets made by Halbwachs (1912), who criticises Le Play for his concentration on supposedly typical cases to the neglect of the full range of variation that could be shown to exist.

target population. Fieldworkers were then required to follow certain routes within the secondary units and to select for interview not individuals who were 'typical' but rather those who would, in the light of the fieldworker's own knowledge, best represent the whole range of social variation existing within the unit. When the survey was completed, its degree of success in producing 'a true miniature' could be gauged, Kiaer (1903) believed, by comparing the distributions of respondents on various 'control variables', such as age, marital status and occupation, with established census distributions.

However, while population sampling as developed by Kiaer marked a clear advance in partial studies, his approach still did not provide a final solution to the problem of generalising from part to whole: that is, from sample to population. Statisticians more versed in the emerging probability theory of the day than was Kiaer pointed out that he did not consider whether discrepancies revealed by his checks through control variables were or were not greater than could be expected by chance; and, further, that even if such checks appeared satisfactory in regard to univariate distributions, this result would not necessarily extend to joint distributions (see further Kruskal and Mosteller, 1980; Lie, 2002).[3]

The solution to the part–whole problem in the context of sample surveys came in fact only with what could be regarded as a further, still more significant advance in population thinking. This was the development, in the place of purposive sampling, of probabilistic, or 'random', sampling. With this approach, the key requirement was that every individual in the target population should be given

---

[3] This last point was in fact made by von Bortkiewicz at a meeting of the International Statistical Institute in 1901 (Kruskal and Mosteller, 1980), and again later in a critique of Max Weber's research on industrial workers in Germany (Verein für Sozialpolitik, 1912). This study by Weber (1908), and another he earlier made of agrarian workers east of the Elbe (Weber, 1892), could be regarded, along with Charles Booth's (1889–1903) study of poverty in London, as ones that sought to bridge the gap between censuses and monographs, but without setting out any underlying rationale for moving from part to whole – or at least not one that could be generally applied.

an equal probability of being selected in the sample or – in later, more sophisticated formulations – a probability that was calculable and not zero. An important pioneer of probabilistic sampling was A. L. Bowley (1906; see also Bowley and Burnett-Hurst, 1915), and chiefly from his work a new conception of representativeness in a sample emerged. Under this new conception, the aim in sampling was not directly to produce 'a true miniature' of the target population, as Kiaer had sought to do, but rather to produce, through probabilistic methods, a sample that was representative or 'fair' in the sense of being *unbiased*, along with some estimation of the error likely to result in making inferences from a probabilistic sample even in the absence of bias.

For some time after the First World War, the old and the new forms of sampling did in fact remain in a state of uneasy coexistence. But the decisive contribution eventually came from none other than Neyman, with whom this book began. In a classic paper, Neyman (1934) gave a compelling demonstration, on both theoretical and empirical grounds, of the dangers of purposive sampling and of the advantages of probabilistic sampling and the calculation of 'confidence intervals' in moving from sample to population. Also important was Neyman's demonstration of how prior knowledge of the target population, which had played a large role in purposive sampling, could be properly brought into sample design: that is, in informing not the selection of sampling units but rather the initial 'stratification' of the target population into subpopulations believed to differ in ways relevant to the purposes of the survey, each of which could then be sampled probabilistically, and with, if desired, differing sampling fractions.[4]

---

[4] Its apparent disregard for all prior population knowledge was something that, at an intuitive level, would appear to have told against probabilistic sampling in the debates of the interwar years. Neyman (1952: 122) at a later point revealed that he himself had wondered 'how would this random sampling work in practice'. He was reassured by its trial application, under his guidance, in a study of the structure of

Post-Neyman, it could be said, the need for the probabilistic sampling of populations in social research became progressively accepted. Proponents of all forms of non-probabilistic sampling have been forced into increasingly defensive positions (Smith, 1997). For example, forms of quota sampling, though still used in market research and political polling (despite well-known disasters, such as in the British General Election of 1992 and again in that of 2015), would now rarely be thought appropriate for serious social scientific research. The basic consideration is that if a sample is *not* selected probabilistically, the non-negligible possibility always exists that the actual procedures involved will themselves be a source of bias: that is, because they will in some way 'tap into' social regularities existing within the target population, so that information is more likely to be obtained from members of this population who possess certain characteristics than from others.[5]

Desrosières (1991, 1993: ch. 7 esp.), in reviewing much the same history as in the foregoing, has represented monographs – or, in modern terminology, case studies – and sample surveys as two different methods of social data collection, each with its own inherent 'logic' of moving from part to whole, which reflect different ways of

the Polish working class undertaken by Jan Pieckalkiewicz (1934). Neyman's (1952) *Lectures and Conferences on Mathematical Statistics and Probability* is dedicated to the memory of Pieckalkiewicz, murdered by the Gestapo in 1943, and to Neyman's other former colleagues in Warsaw who died in the Second World War.

[5] Thus, with quota samples, an initial problem is that of how well the configuration of the sample – the 'quotas' – matches that of the population on the control variables selected. But a further problem is that of how far, in meeting the quotas, the practice of taking substitutes for those individuals who refuse to be interviewed – which is often up to half of those approached – creates an 'availability bias'. Such a bias would appear to have been a major factor in the failure of the polls at the 1992 British General Election. In some cases, it should be added, the very nature of the research problem being addressed may mean that the probabilistic sampling of a target population is not practical and other methods have therefore to be used: as, for example, with the 'snowball' sampling of populations that are 'hidden' because, say, of their members' deviant or subversive activities (Salganik and Heckathorn, 2004) or with the sampling required in social network research where the aim is to go beyond 'ego-centered' to 'complete' networks. But what is important is that in such cases the attempt is then made to evaluate the sample obtained against the 'gold standard' that probabilistic sampling provides.

envisaging human societies: in fact, those expressed in the holistic and the individualistic paradigms, as discussed in Chapters 2 and 3. The increasing dominance of survey methodology, Desrosières then maintains, has to be understood as reflecting macro-social changes, such as the emergence of popular democracies and mass consumer markets. However, such an 'externalist' account of the scientific developments in question, apart from depending on a large measure of quite conjectural history, is seriously deficient in neglecting what would be the focus of an 'internalist' account: that is, the processes through which successive problems were recognised, addressed and overcome. If two different 'logics' of moving from part to whole were indeed involved, then one – that deriving from the individualistic paradigm – was shown, on the basis of evidence and analysis, to be superior to the other – that deriving from the holistic paradigm. And, to revert to the starting point of this chapter, this could in itself be taken as a sufficient explanation of why surveys, with probabilistic sample selection, have become 'the principle means of obtaining information' on human populations: that is, simply because they are the way of undertaking partial studies of these populations, in all their heterogeneity, that can provide the most cogent rationale for moving from part to whole. Such an internalist understanding of the dominance of survey methodology in social research does, moreover, carry wider implications in at least two respects.

First of all, it underlines the fact that the difficulty experienced by the Leplaysians of how to demonstrate the typicality of monographs, or case studies, as a basis for generalising from them has never been resolved. And it is in turn difficult not to see this as the main factor underlying the declining popularity in sociology today of case studies, at least as a means of characterising the populations within which they are situated.

As an illustration here, one may take the rather rapid fall-off that occurred in the number of 'community studies' undertaken in British sociology following a period from the 1930s through to the 1960s, in which they were – as also in the US and elsewhere – among the most prominent forms of social research. What could be regarded as a turning-point in Britain came with the attempt made by Ronald Frankenberg, a disciple of Gluckman (see p. 29), to draw on a selection of community studies in order to 'generalize grandly' about British society 'as a whole' (Frankenberg, 1966: 11–12). Frankenberg's integrative idea was that of a 'morphological' – in effect a rural–urban – continuum of types of community that related primarily to the degree of role differentiation among their inhabitants. But, as well as being of questionable relevance to many of the communities to which Frankenberg sought to apply it, this idea clearly failed to provide a convincing grounding for any wider synthesis. In a subsequent collection of papers on community studies, in part querying their future (Bell and Newby, 1974), little reference was made to Frankenberg's work, and then only critically. What is in this way pointed up is – to echo Kiaer's criticism of the monographers – the error of supposing that typological thinking can be adequate to capture the actual range of population heterogeneity. What undermined Frankenberg's generalising ambitions was not only the increasing variation expressed in the steady emergence of new types of community in post-war Britain – for example, 'bimodal' villages in part colonised by urban commuters, inner-city localities characterised by ethnic divisions and conflict, and 'gentrified' former working-class districts. Far more serious was the quite overlooked variation represented in the social lives of the large numbers of individuals resident in urban and suburban areas in which the very existence of communities of the spatially well-defined kind on which Frankenberg's typology depended would have to be seen as highly problematic.

It may in this connection be further noted that Yin, the author of what is perhaps now the leading text on case-study methodology, explicitly states, in some contrast to positions taken up by earlier authors, that case studies should *not* be regarded as being generalisable in a statistical sense: that is, to populations (Yin, 2003: 10). And, in similar vein, Morgan (2014: 298) acknowledges that there are no systematic rules available, analogous to those used in statistical work, 'for inferring – or transporting – findings beyond the single case study (or even beyond two or three such case studies that suggest the same results)'. Yin, it should be added, goes on to argue that case studies *can* be generalised, if not to populations, then to 'theoretical propositions' (2003: 10). What this means is not entirely clear. But if what is being claimed is that case studies can take on wider significance where they serve as a means of illustrating or, better, of *testing* theoretical propositions *in relation to which their selection has been specifically made* – for example, as in some sense 'deviant' or 'critical' cases – then the argument clearly carries force. It is at all events with this kind of purpose in mind that, in the context of sociology as a population science, case studies could be most appropriately and usefully undertaken (see further Chapter 9).[6]

The second implication of an internalist understanding of why survey research has become dominant in sociology is the following. Any methodology that is to prove capable of superseding, or even supplementing, survey research must itself incorporate the demonstrated advantages of such research in the study of human populations. This point is relevant in regard to arguments now sometimes put forward, usually from externalist positions, to suggest that the age of social surveys is passing, and in particular as a result of the growing possibilities offered to social science by 'big data'.

For example, Savage and Burrows (2007) have claimed that, with the generation and accumulation of vast quantities of 'transactional' data, especially within the private, commercial sector, the privileged role of the sample survey as a means of obtaining information on human populations is being called into question. In comparison with transactional data-gathering, the sample survey is, in their view, 'a

---

[6] As a graduate student in sociology, I was given as a prime example of deviant case analysis the study of democracy within the International Typographical Union by Lipset, Trow and Coleman (1956) – that is, in relation to Michels' 'iron law of oligarchy'. This work was then an influence on the design of the Affluent Worker study in which I was later involved, which took relatively well-paid workers in the rapidly growing industrial town of Luton as providing a critical case for testing the thesis of progressive working-class *embourgeoisement* (Goldthorpe et al., 1969).

very poor instrument', and is in fact unlikely to remain 'a particularly important research tool' (Savage and Burrows, 2007: 891–2).[7]

However, what is here rather remarkably ignored is the extent of the deficiencies that, from a social science standpoint, are apparent in transactional data, as indeed in most other forms of big data, whether resulting from commercial or other – for example, social media – activity (Couper, 2013). To begin with, problems of sample selection bias and thus of representativeness must be expected to arise from the very processes through which big data are generated; and where claims are made that sampling issues do not arise since 'all' cases are covered, further problems are then often apparent regarding the 'all'. That is to say, the population reference lacks clarity or is of doubtful social science relevance. Still more seriously, though, big data-sets usually include only a rather limited range of variables, and then ones relating to the concerns underlying the data-creation process and only coincidentally to sociological concepts or theory. And, in turn, the analysis of such data is typically aimed, as big data enthusiasts do indeed emphasise (see e.g. Mayer-Schönberger and Cukier, 2013: chs 1–4), at making relative short-term *predictions* in regard to some particular outcome, on the basis of entirely inductive, correlational pattern-seeking, with little regard for the need to proceed from the empirically established regularities to causal *explanations*. The dangers in this approach, even for the limited purposes in question, should be evident enough; and, indeed, some initially much-publicised 'successes', such as the Google Flu Trends project, have turned out, on closer examination, to be seriously flawed (Lazer et al., 2014).

Whatever value big data may have for 'knowing capitalism', its value to social science has, therefore, for the present at least, to

---

[7] In direct criticism of survey research, Savage and Burrows put forward only one pertinent point: that it currently faces a problem of declining, and possibly increasingly biased, response rates. However, they then say nothing of the significant advances that have recently been made in addressing this problem through methods of weighting for non-response or for the multiple imputation of missing data.

remain very much open to question. Sociologists should, of course, be ready to use data of whatever provenance if their own purposes can in this way be well served. Some relatively early forms of big data, such as the national registers in Nordic countries, which provide comprehensive information on individuals' incomes or education, are extremely valuable resources that are already widely exploited. But what authors such as Savage and Burrows fail to see is that little will be achieved in drawing on data that fall short of standards that have been established for good scientific reasons. Issues of the quality of data and their fitness for purpose cannot be overlooked. As Cox and Donnelly (2011: 3) aptly put it, 'A large amount of data is in no way synonymous with a large amount of information'. And, indeed, where large data-sets of low quality are analysed, and especially by inductive, 'data-dredging' methods, the risk of *negative* outcomes is high: that is, of noise being mistaken for signal (Silver, 2012) and of essentially arbitrary and thus quite misleading results being produced.[8]

Finally here, it should be noted that, far from there being any actual indications of sample survey research entering into a period of decline, what is at the present time striking is the increasing amount of such research being undertaken and the growing sophistication of survey design and implementation. Moreover, among the most important advances being made are ones that in effect undermine standard criticism of survey research, especially as put forward from holistic positions, to the effect that the conception of society that such research entails is unduly atemporal and atomistic.[9]

---

[8] It is in fact on essentially these lines that cogent criticism (Mills, 2014) has been directed against efforts led by Savage (Savage et al., 2013) to construct a 'new social class map' for Britain on the basis of highly biased big data from self-selected respondents to an internet survey – supplemented by data from a quota-sample survey whose degree of representativeness is not open to any reliable estimation.

[9] For a review of, and a powerful response to, such criticisms, written at the height of the 'reaction against positivism', see the courageous book of Cathie Marsh (1982), whose tragically early death robbed survey research in Britain of one of its rising stars.

On the one hand, the development over recent decades both of repeated cross-sectional surveys of the same population and of longitudinal or panel surveys of the same samples of individuals has become of prime importance *to the understanding of processes of social change*. In particular, longitudinal surveys are crucial to the complex task of separating out the influence on individual life-courses exerted by period, birth-cohort and age or life-cycle effects; or, in other words, to meeting the requirement of Wright Mills (1959) – a one-time strident adversary of survey research – that a key focus of sociological inquiry should be on the intersection of history and biography. And a general feature of analyses based on survey data of the kind in question is their demonstration of how, through these differing effects, a remarkable diversity in individuals' life-courses is created (see e.g. Ferri, Bynner and Wadsworth, 2003) – fully justifying the argument of Wrong (see p. 24) that such diversity is always likely to represent a powerful countervailing force against the homogenising tendencies of enculturation and socialisation.

On the other hand, hierarchical survey designs, in which supra-individual entities are first sampled, and then individuals within these entities, specifically allow for the operation of 'contextual' effects on individuals' life-chances and life-choices: that is, the effects of the social composition and structure of the groups, networks, organisations, associations, communities and so forth in which they are involved. And, in turn, such designs make it possible for the importance of contextual effects to be assessed in comparison with those of individuals' own, variable, characteristics.

In case studies of holistic inspiration, it is often simply assumed that contextual effects are pervasive. For example, such an assumption underpinned much of the work of the Institute of Community Studies in London in the 1950s and 1960s. As Platt (1971: 75–7, 96–8 esp.) has observed, the social class composition of local communities was represented as in various respects shaping the lives of their individual members – but without the question even being considered of whether, or to what extent, such contextual effects could actually be demonstrated independently of the effects of individuals' own class positions.[10] However, in research based on hierarchical survey designs, while contextual effects are usually shown up to some extent in relation to outcomes of interest, they are most often found to be clearly *less* important than are those of individual-level variables – as, say, in the case of school effects on children's academic performance; or, otherwise, contextual effects prove to be difficult to separate out from individual *selection* effects – as, say, in the case of constituency or neighbourhood effects on voting behaviour. In this latter connection, it is also relevant to note that, of late, the inadequate treatment of selection effects has become the focus of criticism (see e.g. Lyons, 2011) of the extreme claims made by some social network analysts that networks exert 'amazing power' over individuals' lives and operate as 'a kind of human superorganism' (Christakis and Fowler, 2010: xii). The crucial question that arises is that of how far their networks influence individuals or how far individuals choose and thus influence their networks.[11]

The main concern of this chapter has been to show that probabilistic sample surveys represent a statistically informed methodology that is foundational for sociology as a population science: that is, because such surveys constitute the best means so far devised of moving from part to whole when trading off population coverage against informational content in the collection of data from human

---

[10] More recently, unsupported assumptions on similar lines can be found in literature in which the individual risk of poverty or 'social exclusion' is associated with the contextual effects of living in inner-city districts or 'sink' estates.

[11] Lyons' particular concern is with the claim made by Christakis and Fowler that the influence of social network membership increases the risk of obesity. A more general issue of the existence or strength of contextual effects in regard to health and well-being also arises in debates over the work of Wilkinson and Pickett (2010): that is, over their argument that the adverse effects of economic inequality operate not only at the individual level but also, and more importantly, at the societal level. Research reviews indicating that the evidence for such contextual effects is, at best, patchy (e.g. Lynch et al., 2004; Leigh, Jencks and Smeeding, 2009) have received no serious response from Wilkinson and Pickett, and the bivariate scatterplots on which they largely rely are of little help in supporting their case: analyses based on appropriate hierarchical survey designs and multilevel modelling are called for.

populations. In the light of the foregoing, it can, however, also be said that the advance of survey methodology has *in itself* significantly aided the development of population thinking, as opposed to typological thinking, in sociology. In particular, awareness has been increased of the degree of individual variation, especially where a life-course perspective is taken, and of the limits on the extent to which this variation is modified by individuals' involvement in supra-individual entities. It is in this regard of interest to note a comment made by the author of a leading text on the modelling of data from more sophisticated survey designs. Hox (2010: 8) observes that, while Durkheim's conception of sociology was as a science 'that focuses primarily on the constraints that a society can put on its members', there are now good grounds for some reversal of perspective: that is, for a focus on the extent to which the features of sociocultural entities are shaped by the actions of the individuals by whom they are, or once were, populated.

7   Statistics and methods of data analysis

In sociology as a population science the foundational role played by statistics in establishing population regularities stems, in the second place, from the need for methods of data analysis that are able to demonstrate the presence and the form of the population regularities that are emergent from the variability of human social life.

In this chapter, I move on from the role played by statistics in informing methods of data collection in sociology as a population science – that is, through sample survey research – to the role statistics plays in informing data analysis – that is, through what has become known as 'multivariate analysis'. In fact, close links exist in the social sciences between sample survey research and multivariate data analysis; they have to a large extent evolved together.

In order to use surveys to capture the degree of variability in human social life or, in other words, population heterogeneity, the nature of this heterogeneity, or of such part of it as is of research interest, must be specified: that is to say, variables must be envisaged. This entails, to revert to the discussion of Chapter 5, the formation of appropriate concepts and then the development of classifications or scales through which these concepts can be made operational as variables with an adequate degree of reliability and validity. In turn, data from survey research expressed in variable form become the material to which methods of multivariate analysis can be applied in order to bring out – to make visible – the perhaps quite complex relations existing among variables. And it is through the statistical modelling of social data in this way that, in the manner suggested by Stigler, the objects of study of sociology are formed: the population regularities emergent from individual variability that constitute appropriate sociological explananda.

The term 'variable sociology' has often been used pejoratively in attacks on quantitative sociology, whether from 'anti-positivist' or other positions. It is, however, important to note that two quite different lines of criticism arise, although they are not infrequently confounded.

One objection (see e.g. Abbott, 1992; Esser, 1996; Sørensen, 1998) is concerned with the way in which, in sociological analysis conducted in terms of relations among variables, the action and inter-action of individuals that underlie these relations can be, and often are, lost from sight. Thus, not only the description of social regulari-ties *but also their explanation* is given at the level of variables: that is to say, explanation takes the form simply of showing how far the dependent variable of an analysis can be statistically 'accounted for' by those variables deemed to be independent. It is, in other words, vari-ables rather than individuals that 'do the acting'. This argument is one with which I am in essential agreement, and I return to it in Chapter 8.

A second objection is of a more radical but, I believe, far less compelling kind. This objection goes back at least to Blumer (1956) and is to the effect that thinking in terms of variables is inadequate in that much of what is important in human social life cannot be 'reduced' to variable form, even for purposes of description. In part, this critique relies simply on examples of what could be accepted as bad practice in variable sociology: inadequate conceptualisation, deficiencies in the way concepts are made operational and so on. But insofar as it is to be regarded as a critique in principle, it suffers from one major weakness: namely, that its proponents have been unable to offer any alternative to the language of variables as a means of describing features of human social life. It is indeed difficult to envisage any alternative, and this point is underlined by the fact that in qualitative just as in quantitative sociological work, one finds that the language of variables is quite routinely, if only implicitly, resorted to, and further that multivariate analysis is in effect often attempted, albeit at only a verbal level.[1]

---

[1] Insofar as in qualitative work concepts are not translated explicitly into variables with due concern for reliability and validity, as is a requirement in quantitative work (see Chapter 5), two further consequences may be noted. First, the absence of

'Variable sociology' has then to be regarded as the best, if not the only, way available of producing descriptions of probabilistic population regularities; and its consequent importance is well brought out in a late paper by Robert Merton (1987: 2–6) under the rubric of 'establishing the phenomena'. What Merton is concerned with is the need, before proceeding further in sociological analysis, to ensure that two requirements are met.

The first requirement is that it should be clear that some social regularity does indeed exist – or, as Merton puts it, that events of a certain kind have 'enough of a regularity to *require* and *allow* explanation' (1987: 2–6; italics added). Both words that I have emphasised are significant. To go back to the position I took up in Chapter 4, events that do not display regularity do not call for the sociologist's attention: they are not appropriate sociological explananda, and seeking to explain them sociologically will not be rewarding.

The second requirement then is that every effort should be made to ensure that the form of the regularity in question is properly understood. What at first sight appears to be a fairly straightforward regularity may well, on closer examination, turn out to be a more complex one.

Merton develops his argument by giving various examples of supposed social regularities that, in the light of further research, proved to be non-existent or to have been misconstrued, and he takes the occasion to reassert a view he had expressed two decades previously: that a concern with establishing the phenomena should not be dismissed as 'mere empiricism' since 'pseudo-facts have a way of inducing pseudo-problems, which cannot be solved because matters are not what they purport to be' (Merton, 1959: xv).[2]

this discipline makes it much easier for slippage in meanings and usages to occur. Second, it becomes difficult, if not impossible, for empirical findings to be placed in the public domain in a form that would allow others to reanalyse them – in the way that data-sets resulting from quantitative research are now placed in data archives, together with appropriate documentation, as a matter of course.

[2] I recall once hearing much the same warning being given, in more colourful fashion, by Bill Sewell: 'before you come up with some smart explanation of how the pig got into the tree, just be sure that it *is* the pig that is in the tree'.

Seeking to meet Merton's requirements through multivariate data analysis – that is, using such analysis in the attempt to demonstrate the presence of associations or correlations among variables and to express these relationships in a valid rather than a 'spurious' form – has in fact for long been a central concern of quantitative sociology. In the period after the Second World War, for example, such a concern figured prominently in the work of the group around Paul Lazarsfeld – a close colleague of Merton – at the Bureau of Applied Social Research at Columbia (see e.g. Kendall and Lazarsfeld, 1950; Lazarsfeld, 1955). In analysing contingency tables derived primarily from social survey data, Lazarsfeld and his associates typically began with bivariate relationships and then sought to 'elaborate' these through the introduction of third and further variables, whether in the role of antecedent, mediating or possibly confounding variables.

Lazarsfeld himself saw such elaboration, especially when linked with the time-ordering of variables, as being directed towards demonstrating causation, or at least potential causation. However, his procedures could be better taken as having an essentially descriptive value: that is, as a means of reliably establishing explananda rather than of providing explanations in causal terms. And this did in fact become increasingly evident by the 1970s, as the Lazarsfeldian approach to the analysis of contingency tables was developed and superseded by more formal and powerful loglinear modelling and related methods, notably on the basis of the work of Leo Goodman.[3] Such modelling

---

[3] A further valuable descriptive technique for sociologists, latent class analysis – in effect the categorical counterpart of factor analysis for continuous variables – was also pioneered by Lazarsfeld (see esp. Lazarsfeld and Henry, 1968); and this too can be understood as closely related to loglinear modelling (McCutcheon and Mills, 1998). In view of criticisms earlier made of typological thinking in sociology, it should be added here that, where typologies are constructed on the basis of latent class analysis – or of optimal matching techniques, as discussed later in this chapter – they can be regarded, in contrast to *a priori* or 'ideal' types, simply as empirical findings: that is, as in themselves a form of revealed population regularity. For it is an important feature of the techniques in question that, where properly used, they may well lead to a negative conclusion: that is, indicate that no regularity in the form of a manageable typology is to be found.

explicitly focuses on revealing patterns of association – and including, perhaps, quite complex interactions – among variables in multi-way contingency tables without any causal implications being claimed and indeed without any need arising for variables to be distinguished as dependent or independent. As Goodman (2007a: 16) has put it in a retrospective paper, what is in this way chiefly contributed is the possibility of bringing out – making visible – for further study regularities of a hitherto unrecognised kind: that is, regularities that were previously 'hidden, embedded in a block of dense data'.

To give a specific illustration of this latter point, I may turn to what was, for a time, a controversial issue in British electoral sociology, in which I had myself some passing involvement: that is, the issue of the role played by gender in political party support. Polling data collected prior to British General Elections from 1945 through at least to the 1980s consistently revealed that the percentage-point difference in Conservative versus Labour support favoured the Conservatives to a greater extent among women than among men. Commentators, especially from the left – a notable example being Hart (1989) – were then led to argue that this 'gender gap' revealed Labour's lack of concern with women's interests and a preoccupation with inequalities and exploitation associated with social class rather than with gender. If Labour had appealed to women to the same extent as to men, it was claimed, the party would have won all elections in the period in question. In other words, the gender gap was explained by a specifically gender effect: that stemming from what Hart (1989) refers to as Labour politicians' 'masculinist blinkers'.

However, while a gender gap in voting could indeed be regularly observed, the nature of the regularity was not in fact well understood until more detailed survey data than those provided by the polling agencies became available. On this basis, the bivariate relationship between gender and vote could be 'elaborated' through multivariate analyses that brought in the further factors of class and of age. And what these analyses then indicated was that the gender gap was a regularity far more complex in its form than had initially appeared. It was in fact largely an epiphenomenon of *other regularities in which gender-linked voting was not involved*. In responding to a further paper by Hart (1994), I investigated patterns of association in a four-way contingency table of sex × age × class × vote at the 1964 General Election by applying a series of loglinear models (Goldthorpe, 1994) and was able to show that this table was well fitted by a model proposing two three-way associations: that is, of sex, age and class and of age, class and vote. When a further association between sex and vote was added to this model, the improvement in fit was not significant. In other words, the gender gap could be seen as the outcome, on the one hand, of the tendency of women to live longer than men, and especially women in more advantaged classes; and, on the other hand, of the tendency for older people, and especially older people in more advantaged classes, to be more likely to vote Conservative than Labour. A focus on the simple bivariate association that was most immediately in evidence could therefore be seriously misleading. Although over the period in question women *were* more likely than men to favour the Conservatives, multivariate analysis revealed that to seek to explain this regularity in terms of a gender effect – such as Labour's 'masculinist blinkers' – was to grapple with a Mertonian 'pseudo-problem'.[4]

It may, however, be added that my own and others' analyses of what exactly was involved in the gender gap in voting did at the same time serve to reveal one further, quite genuine problem: that is, one concerning the effect of age on voting and the implications of this for the gender gap. The question clearly emerged of whether the age effect was to be understood in life-cycle terms – people tend to become politically more conservative as they get older – or rather in birth-cohort, or 'political generation' terms. Subsequent research, based on repeated surveys of the British electorate, has in fact given strong support to the latter interpretation. And, consistently with this, as

---

[4] This is not, of course, to say that no such blinkers existed – only that, if they did exist, they were of little relevance in explaining the existing gender gap in voting.

individuals born in the earlier twentieth century have died out, so too has the gender gap in party support that previously existed – and with, if anything, a gap opening up in the reverse direction. The question does of course again arise of whether any such reversal itself results specifically from a gender effect or from other factors. But the need to go beyond the simple bivariate association to establish the precise form of the explanandum is now well appreciated by researchers in the field (see e.g. Inglehart and Norris, 2003: ch. 4).

As, then, contingency table analysis has evolved, its prime importance in sociology as a means of providing descriptions – although perhaps quite sophisticated descriptions – rather than explanations of population regularities has become generally recognised. Loglinear modelling and related methods are now routinely applied in this way in many areas of sociological research: for example, apart from electoral sociology, in the study of social mobility, of social class, gender and ethnic inequalities in educational attainment, and of patterns of homogamy and heterogamy.

However, what has then also to be recognised is that, in the case of regression analysis – the most widely used form of multivariate analysis in sociology – a tendency has of late become evident for this likewise to be seen not as a method of obtaining causal explanations of social phenomena but, again, as one that best serves to establish and describe them. Thus, in a current text on regression analysis, intended primarily for social scientists, one can in fact find the author explicitly stating – in marked contrast to what would have been expected over preceding decades – that regression should be understood as 'inherently a descriptive tool' (Berk, 2004: 206). And what is in turn of further interest in the present context is that it is possible to trace out a reasoned connection between this development and the understanding of sociology as a population science.

For early proponents of regression analysis in sociology, such as Blalock (1961), it was its apparent potential as a means of moving 'from association to causation' (see Freedman, 1997) in research fields largely reliant on observational rather than experimental data that was its prime attraction. In Chapter 8, I am concerned to show how this understanding of the use of regression has subsequently met with mounting criticism from both statisticians and sociologists alike, and would seem by now to have rather few – overt – supporters. Here, though, I wish to bring out the more positive side of the situation: that is, the way in which an alternative and far more sustainable view of the role of regression in sociology has emerged, and one that would today seem to be very widely adopted in research, at all events *de facto*.

The difference between the two approaches to the use of regression that are in question here is illuminatingly set out in a paper by Xie (2007). Xie emphasises that, with both approaches, regression is the same statistical operation – but that crucial differences arise in the objectives pursued, in underlying assumptions and in the interpretation of the results that are obtained. Blalock and those following him, Xie argues, adhered to what may be called a 'Gaussian' conception of regression. In this case, the aim is to establish a law-like causal relationship between what are taken to be the independent and the dependent variables of the analysis, and the deviation of individual observations from this relationship is then in effect treated as measurement error: that is, as simply undesirable noise. Blalock can thus be regarded as a quantitative analyst much in the style of Quetelet, with, as it were, the least-squares solution of the regression equation replacing the average as the focus of scientific interest; or, in other words, as Xie suggests, Blalock was essentially a 'typological thinker' (Xie, 2007).

In contrast, Xie identifies a 'Galtonian' conception of regression, which he associates primarily with the work of Dudley Duncan, pre-eminently a 'population thinker' (Xie, 2007). In this case, the aim of regression is not to determine causal relationships but rather, through the coefficients returned, to provide a parsimonious description of population variability in regard to the outcome with which the analysis is concerned. The focus is on the systematic component of this variability: that is, on the variability that occurs among the groups of sociological interest that are defined by the independent variables of the analysis. But it is at the same time understood that the error term of the equation will reflect real *within-group* variability, apart from measurement error *stricto sensu*. And, while of course attempts always can – and should – be made to elaborate the model so as to increase that part of the variability that can be treated as socially systematic, it has to be accepted that within-group, individual-level variability will always remain substantial.[5]

What may then be noted here is the affinity that exists, in regard to data analysis, between regression in this Galtonian sense and the individualistic paradigm in sociology – an affinity that runs parallel to that previously discussed, in regard to data collection, between sample survey research and this paradigm. In both cases alike, the source of the affinity lies in an awareness of the high degree of variability that exists in human social life at the individual level – that is, of population heterogeneity – and of the need for research methods that can be fully responsive to this variability while at the same time allowing the demonstration of such regularities as may exist within it.

It is in this perspective that one should in turn understand the point that is several times made by Duncan that no great importance can attach to the absolute size of the R^2s that are returned by

[5] Given Duncan's pioneering work in 'causal path' analysis in sociology and his later text on structural equation modelling (Duncan, 1975), it might be thought strange that he should be represented as standing in opposition to Blalock's position. However, as Xie (2007) documents, Duncan always emphasised the limitations of such techniques, especially in regard to the demonstration of causation. Xie also reports that Duncan informed him of the difficulties he had in correspondence with Blalock in getting across his views on sociology as a population science (Xie, 2007: 146). Duncan's correspondence – in this case with David Freedman – is of further interest as the apparent source of the distinction between Gaussian and Galtonian conceptions of regression (Xie, 2007: 145, 147). The shifting influence of the methodological work of Lazarsfeld, Duncan and Goodman on American sociology is hilariously captured in the 'anonymous document' reprinted in Goodman (2007b: 137), which should be introductory reading for all sociology students following courses in data analysis.

regression analyses in sociology – these being, with any sensible model, rarely much above 0.3.[6] While, under the holistic paradigm, as already remarked, the expectation would be that far more of population variance than this should be capable of being systematically accounted for, under the individualistic paradigm what is perhaps most remarkable is that regression analyses are usually able to show up *some* systematic effects – despite the fact that the data being analysed will, as Achen (1982: 13) has commented, derive from 'a hopeless jumble of human actors' all engaging to some degree in 'idiosyncratic behaviour as a function of numberless distinctive features of their histories and personalities'. Duncan himself observes, with apparent reference to unmet 'holistic' expectations, that, while the institutional and other structural features of a society may well serve to modify variability in a number of individual characteristics, this will still be 'not nearly so large as the number on which individuals actually differ' (Duncan, 1975: 166–7). And he then goes on pointedly to ask – in what might be regarded as a Malinowskian spirit (see pp. 26–7) – if those sociologists who despair of their low R^2s would 'care to live in the society so structured' that their particular collection of variables 'accounts for 90% instead of 32% of the variance in Y' (Duncan, 1975: 167).

If, then, it is the case that, in sociology as a population science, regression analysis should be seen as serving to establish probabilistic population regularities – in essentially the same way as explicitly descriptive techniques such as loglinear modelling and its derivatives – one further question rather directly arises and needs, in conclusion, to be addressed. That is, the question of whether, in their descriptive work, sociologists should make greater use than they

---

[6] By 'sensible' here is meant a model that does not include an independent variable that is so 'close' to the dependent variable as to make the analysis essentially uninformative. For example, in a regression model with individuals' social class position at time t as the dependent variable, a high R^2 could of course be achieved by including as an independent variable class position at $t - 1$ week.

presently do of statistical methods that, rather than being based on an explicit probabilistic model of some kind, rely on purely algorithmic modelling – in effect on 'machine learning' from the data under analysis through the application of various techniques of pattern search. The highly controversial issues that arise here in a general statistical context are well brought out in a paper by Breiman (2001) and subsequent discussion (see esp. Cox, 2001). However, care is needed in moving from this general context to the possibilities for algorithmic modelling in sociology specifically.

What is important to note is that the research contexts in which algorithmic modelling has so far been most effectively applied often differ significantly from those most likely to obtain in sociology. Either they are ones in which the aim is to provide short-term predictions of practical importance from given, although often big, data (see the discussion in Chapter 6) – as, say, regarding daily ozone levels or risks of motorway congestion – and where, thus, predictive accuracy takes clear precedence over the interpretability of the results produced. Or they are ones in which it is possible for the algorithmic search to be given strong theoretical guidance – as, say, in the analysis of DNA sequences through optimal matching (OM) techniques. In sociology, by contrast, there is usually the possibility of designing data collection, through survey methods, with specific research problems in mind, and the main aim is in any event not individual-level prediction – that is, high R^2s – but rather to establish the correct form of such population-level regularities as may be present. But, at the same time, strong theory through which pattern search could be informed may well be lacking. While, therefore, there is no reason for sociologists to reject algorithmic modelling out of hand, it would, at least for the present, seem wise to resort to it only on the basis of a detailed evaluation of its likely advantages and disadvantages in particular cases.

For purposes of illustration here, one could take the use of OM (as pioneered in sociology by Abbott: see esp. Abbott and Tsay,

2000), and specifically its use in various aspects of life-course research (as insightfully discussed by Billari, 2005). In treating regularities in events within the life-course, such as occur in the formation and dissolution of partnerships and families or in entry into and exit from employment, and in particular in analysing the correlates of the occurrence and timing of such events, panel regression and event history modelling have come to play a central role. However, as Billari observes, it is difficult through such methods to envisage life-course events as forming 'total' sequences, or trajectories, rather than as being stochastically generated from one time-point to another. And a total view could well be desirable, not least insofar as individuals may themselves envisage their life-courses in this way and pursue long-term life-course strategies, albeit ones subject to various constraints and the operation of essential chance. In this regard, then, sequence analysis, as through OM techniques, has obvious attractions. The series of different states constituting some aspect of the life-course can be systematically 'matched', individual by individual, in terms of the extent and kind of changes that would be necessary to make one sequence of states identical to another, and, on this basis, a matrix of distances between all pairs of sequences can be algorithmically generated. In turn, this matrix can serve as input to some further clustering or multidimensional scaling algorithm that can – or at all events, may – yield a manageable empirical set of sequences.

However, as is in fact widely recognised, the major problem that arises here, as with most sociological applications of OM, is that of setting the 'costs' of transforming one sequence of life-course states into another: that is, the costs to be attributed to the required substitution, insertion or deletion of states. Since it is these costs that determine the distances between sequences, via the algorithmic modelling, they are fundamental to the entire OM analysis; and unless they can be given a convincing rationale, the resulting matrix of distances and any typologies of sequences derived from it are open to the charge that, rather than reflecting some actually existing social regularities, they may be quite artefactual (Levine, 2000; Wu, 2000). Various ways of dealing with this problem – in effect, the problem of the validity of OM analyses – have been proposed (for a useful review, see Aisenbrey and Fasang, 2010), but what would seem of key importance is that the treatment of transformation costs should have as clear a theoretical basis as possible. Thus, some of the more persuasive OM analyses have been ones of individuals' worklife and, more specifically, social-class histories, in which transformation costs are derived from the theory underlying well-validated class schemata, such as those referred to in Chapter 5 (e.g. Halpin and Chan, 1998). And in such cases, it may then also be possible, by means, say, of regression analyses, for the emergent types of class histories to be related in theoretically coherent ways to antecedent variables such as social origins, cognitive ability and educational attainment (e.g. Bukodi et al., 2015). However, in many sociological applications of OM, including in life-course research, it has to be said that the choice of transformation costs does still appear arbitrary to a rather disturbing degree.

OM, and likewise other algorithmic modelling methods, could therefore best be regarded as ones of *potential* value to sociologists in their efforts to establish the population regularities that form their basic objects of study – but methods that still need to be used very selectively, and with full awareness of the pitfalls to which they may lead. They should, moreover, be seen as ones that are complementary, or indeed ancillary, to probabilistic modelling, rather than as representing some radical and comprehensive alternative. Claims to the effect that algorithmic modelling, and in particular sequence analysis, marks the end of 'the variables revolution' in empirical sociology and the emergence of a new paradigm that focuses on 'events in context' rather than on 'entities with variable attributes' (Abbott, 1995: 93; Abbott and Tsay, 2000: 24; Aisenbrey and Fasang, 2010: 422) would seem little more than rhetorical flourishes – comparable to those noted previously proclaiming the end of social surveys in the era of big data. Data-driven 'computational' sociology (see Lazer et al., 2009) may well become more prominent. But, far from being superseded, variable sociology in the sense in which it has been understood in this chapter and its expression through probabilistic statistical modelling are, like social survey research, features of sociology that are here for the long term.

8 The limits of statistics: causal explanation

While statistically informed methods of data collection and analysis are foundational in establishing the probabilistic population regularities that constitute sociological explananda, statistical analysis alone cannot lead to causal explanations of these regularities.

In preceding chapters, the emphasis has been on the crucial part played by statistically informed methods of data collection and analysis in forming the objects of study – the proper explananda – of sociology as a population science: that is, probabilistic population regularities. Such methods would appear essential – no viable alternative to them has been demonstrated – as the means of accommodating the variability of human social life, while at the same time enabling regularities within it to be discovered and adequately described. In the present chapter, however, the emphasis changes. It now falls on what statistical methodology by itself *cannot* achieve within sociology, and should not be expected to achieve: that is, the provision of causal explanations of the regularities that this methodology serves to establish. Dudley Duncan (1992: 668) once spoke of sociology's 'Faustian bargain' with statistics; it is some aspects of the darker side of this bargain that have now to be considered.

As noted in Chapter 7, in early applications of multivariate data analysis in sociology it was often supposed that such analyses could not only reveal various regularities of association in social data but also lead to the demonstration of causal relationships. In particular, forms of regression analysis, culminating in causal path modelling, were seen as the prime means of moving from association to causation. However, over recent decades this view has become subject to increasing doubts and criticism from within statistics and sociology alike, and it would by now appear to receive rather little overt support. At most, it might be claimed that regression analyses allow for a 'causal interpretation'.[1]

From the side of statistics, perhaps the most telling interventions have been those of David Freedman (1991, 1992, 1997, 2010). Freedman explicitly rejects the idea that causal relationships can, in any field of research, be cranked out of data on the basis of statistical technique alone. Thus, in the case of regression, he stresses that if a regression model is to be appropriately specified for purposes of causal explanation, a prior subject-matter input is always required regarding the processes by which the data under analysis have actually been generated. This is necessary in order to determine the variables that are to be included in the analysis, their supposed causal ordering, the functional form of the relations between them, the properties of error terms and so on. If the regression model adopted is not consistent with the processes in question – if, to take the most obvious example, a relevant variable is omitted – then all causal inferences drawn from the model will be vitiated. Freedman accepts that the problems that here arise may be less consequential if regression is taken simply as a means of description: that is, as a means of summarising the associations that happen to hold in the data analysed among the variables that are in fact recognised. But if causal inference is the aim of the analysis, the crucial issue that arises is that of whether the regression coefficients returned can be taken to have what Freedman (1997: 117) aptly calls 'a life of their own': that is, outside of the data from which in any particular case they are estimated. This will only be so if the regression model is correctly specified, and only then will counterfactuals implying causation be licensed. In other words, only then

---

[1] A good deal of confusion, or equivocation, is in this regard made possible by the fact that the language in which regression is discussed is permeated with terms with apparent causal implications: 'effects', 'determinants', 'dependence' and so on. It would be difficult at this stage to introduce any alternative terminology, but it would be helpful if more sociologists were to follow the practice of making it clear when they are using such apparently causal language simply as a *façon de parler*. The term 'statistical effects' is sometimes used to indicate that 'causal effects' are not being implied.

will it be possible to claim that if a particular independent variable were to be changed, a corresponding change – of a size indicated by the coefficient for that variable – would be caused in the dependent variable of the analysis.

Freedman (2010: 11–15) illustrates this line of argument with the example of regression analysis as applied in the case of Hooke's Law. This law states the qualitative nature of a relationship: that is, that, up to a limit, the extension of a spring is in direct linear proportion to the load added to it. Using experimental or observational data in order to regress extension on load then serves to quantify the law in the case of a particular spring or type of spring. The law itself reflects the physical process through which the data will have been produced, and the form of the law is in turn embodied in the regression model. In this case, then, a high R^2 can be expected, with the error term reflecting simply measurement error – from, say, deficiencies in the experimental set-up or faulty observation; and the regression coefficient estimated will be interpretable as capturing *a specific property* of the spring or type of spring: that is, as having in this sense a 'life of its own' rather than one conditional on the particular data analysed. In turn, therefore, this coefficient could be used, within a limit, in order to predict what change in the extension of the spring would be caused by a change in load.

Here, one has in fact a clear example of what, following Xie (see pp. 92–3), one could characterise as the Gaussian conception of regression. What has, however, to be recognised is that, in sociology, regression can rarely, if ever, be applied under this conception: the kind of theory exemplified by Hooke's Law is simply not available as a basis. Consider, for example, analyses that, using data for a particular place and time, regress the earnings or occupational status of individuals in different ethnic groups on their levels of educational attainment (with, say, various control variables being also included). What has here to be accepted is, first of all, that there are no strong grounds for supposing that the coefficients estimated will be replicated with data for other places and times – they may or may not be.

But further, and more seriously, it has also to be accepted that if, in the original case, the distribution of education were to change – if, say, educational differences among ethnic groups were to be narrowed – the changes in ethnic differences in earnings or status that would be predicted under the regression model would not necessarily follow. It could just as well be that change would occur *in the regression coefficients themselves*: for example, that the earnings or status returns to education would fall (see Lieberson, 1987: 166–7, 186–8). The underlying problem is that no general and compelling theory exists of the processes whereby such returns to education are actually produced that could guide the specification of the regression model.[2]

A growing realisation of the difficulties involved in seeking to derive causal explanations from regression of the kind highlighted by Freedman is, then, one source of the re-evaluation of regression as essentially a descriptive method that, as noted in the previous chapter, has become evident in sociology – and that in turn lends importance to Xie's argument that a Galtonian rather than a Gaussian conception of regression is that which sociologists do now in fact mostly apply and should explicitly adopt.[3] However, criticism of the idea of moving from association to causation via regression has been made not only from a statistical standpoint but further, and also influentially, from within sociology itself.

What is in this regard notable is the degree to which such criticism has run in parallel to that made by Freedman: that is, in

---

[2] Some economists would appear to believe that, so far as the earnings returns to education are concerned, human capital theory fills the bill. However, how exactly educational attainment is to be related to the concept of human capital and what control variables – such as, say, cognitive ability or various non-cognitive attributes – it is appropriate to introduce appear far from clear. In the evaluation of human capital theory, this then allows, in Blaug's (1992: 218) words, 'the persistent resort to ad hoc auxiliary assumptions to account for every perverse result'.

[3] An important turning-point in this process was perhaps marked by Freedman's (1992) critique of causal path analysis as deployed in Hope (1984), although, as was generally recognised (see Duncan, 1992), this was simply a restatement of an earlier critique of this methodology in Blau and Duncan (1967) that had been widely circulated as a working paper.

emphasising the need for an understanding of the processes that generate the data that are under analysis. While, for Freedman, such an understanding is necessary if a regression model is to be properly specified, for many sociologists, revealing such processes is in fact what establishing causation in sociology essentially entails, independently of any statistical procedures. It is this view that motivates the objection to 'variable sociology', referred to in Chapter 7, that it reduces sociological explanation simply to showing how far dependent variables can be statistically 'accounted for' by those treated as independent, without any attention being given to the social processes that underlie the results obtained. And, at least for sociologists working within the individualistic paradigm, these processes are ones that need to be ultimately understood in terms of the actions and interactions of the individuals involved. Thus, Coleman (1986: 1314–15) has pointed to the paradox that sociologists engaged in 'empirical, statistical survey research' largely analyse individual-level data yet very frequently do so without any explicit reference to the individual action from which these data derive. Likewise, Boudon (1987: 61–2) has objected that in such research it is too often variables rather than individuals that are in effect taken as the units of analysis, and that demonstrations of the statistical effect of one variable on another are considered as 'final results' without any attempt being made to show how these statistical relations derive from their 'real causes', which can lie only in the actions of individuals.

Thus, to revert, for purposes of illustration, to regression analyses of the effects of individuals' education on their earnings or occupational status, what would be maintained from the position taken up by Coleman and Boudon is that if education could, on this basis, be said to 'cause' earnings or occupational status, this could only be in a very elliptical and sociologically uninformative sense. What would be further needed for an adequate demonstration of causation would be some account of why the statistical results come out as they do. For example, some account would be needed, on the one hand, of the processes – involving choice and constraint – through which individuals attain certain educational levels, with perhaps their economic futures in mind (see further pp. 117–19); and, on the other hand, of the processes through which this attainment then conditions their chances of entry, via the actions of employers or their agents, into occupations affording differing levels of earnings or status (Goldthorpe, 2014).

In sum, the argument is, again as with Freedman, that establishing causation cannot result from statistical procedures alone but must be dependent upon some subject-matter theoretical input relating to how the data under analysis are produced. The main difference is that while, for Freedman, causal inference from statistical analysis requires such input from the start, for Coleman and Boudon such input has to follow on from the results of statistical analysis, in themselves essentially descriptive, if a causal explanation is to be provided of the regularities that are demonstrated.

The question of how sociologists can in fact best seek to move from the description to the explanation of population regularities will be the specific concern of Chapter 9. In the remainder of the present chapter, attention needs to be given to a further reaction that has developed within sociology to the ending of 'the age of regression' – but one which would, again, appear to lead to undue expectations about the part that can be played in establishing causation by statistical methodology alone. This reaction derives from a conception of causation that differs significantly from that underlying regression and related forms of analysis, and one which, its proponents would maintain, is of a stronger and 'deeper' kind.

With regression, as indeed with Lazarsfeld's attempts to derive causation from contingency-table analysis, causation is in effect equated with the existence of an association between the dependent variable of the analysis and the independent variable or variables *that can be shown to be robust*: that is, that can be shown to persist when other conceivably explanatory variables are introduced. It is this robust dependence that serves as the evidence that a causal relationship prevails. The main weakness of this understanding of causation is, of course, the difficulty involved in ruling out the possibility that the supposed causal relationship might be shown to be spurious if some further, hitherto unconsidered, perhaps entirely unsuspected factor – a 'lurking' variable – were to be taken into account. The alternative conception of causality that has of late been advocated for sociology seeks to avoid this difficulty. It derives from primarily applied research in such fields as agriculture, medicine and education, where it is possible for experimental or quasi-experimental methods to be pursued and where interest centres on the effectiveness, or otherwise, of some kind of *intervention*.

Under this alternative conception, causation, or a 'causal effect', is understood in terms of *the change that is produced* in a dependent or outcome variable of interest as the result of an intervention or of what is often referred to as a 'treatment'. More specifically, a causal effect is the difference found in the outcome variable as between randomly selected experimental units that receive a treatment and those that do not – that is, that serve as controls: for example, as between crop yields on plots of land given or not given a fertiliser, between the recovery rates of patients given or not given a drug or between the examination results of students subject or not subject to a particular pedagogical method.[4] This difference in outcomes can be quantified by calculating the 'average treatment effect', or some variant thereof, with the counterfactual and causally significant implication then being that, absent the treatment, no such difference would be observed. It is therefore crucial for the applicability of this 'potential outcomes' understanding of causation that an intervention in some form or other should occur – or, at least, could be envisaged as occurring: in Holland's (1986: 958) phrase, 'no causation without manipulation'.[5]

---

[4] The random allocation of units to the treatment or control 'arms' of the experiment is regarded as the crucial means of controlling for all possibly confounding variables, known or unknown.

[5] I have discussed this and other understandings of causation in sociology at greater length in Goldthorpe (2007: vol. 1, ch. 9).

An impressive body of statistical technique has evolved in connection with the potential outcomes approach: not only concerning
the design of experiments to test the effectiveness of interventions –
in particular 'randomised controlled trials' (RCTs) – but further, and
of main relevance for present purposes, concerning the extension of
the approach to non-experimental, observational studies, including
those based on sample surveys of populations (see e.g. Rosenbaum,
1995). In this case, what is in effect entailed is considering these
studies *as if* they were experiments, although ones not carried out
under the control of the researcher, and then seeking means of coun-
teracting the effects of departures from an appropriate experimental
design that could follow from this lack of control. The major work
reviewing these developments from the standpoint of sociology, and
advocating their use by sociologists, is Morgan and Winship (2007).
These authors specifically contrast the potential outcomes approach
to causation with the regression or 'equation-based' approach and see
the latter as being inimical to 'careful thinking about how the data in
hand differ from what would have been generated by the ideal experiments one might wish to have conducted' (Morgan and Winship,
2007: 13).[6]

Taken on its own terms, the line of argument that Morgan and
Winship pursue is a forceful one, and in attempts to develop causal
arguments on the basis of data from observational studies, to adopt

---

[6] Morgan and Winship actually prefer to speak of the 'counterfactual' rather than the
'potential outcomes' approach to causation, and are also clearly influenced by the
work of Pearl (2000), which can be seen as an attempt to re-express and develop the
potential outcomes approach by introducing ideas from computer science, imple-
mented through directed acyclic graphs (DAGs). However, much controversy in this
regard persists. See, for example, the fierce exchanges in *Statistics in Medicine*,
2007–09. For a different approach to the use of DAGs, more consistent with the
understanding of causation to be developed in Chapter 9, see Cox and Wermuth
(1996: 219–27 esp.). These authors regard graphical methods as being able to provide
representations of data that are 'potentially causal' – that is, that are 'consistent with
or suggestive of causal interpretation' – while recognising that causality has itself
to be established in terms of some 'underlying process or mechanism' derived from
theory in substantive research areas.

the standpoint of experimental design may often provide a valuable discipline. However, the potential outcomes approach has not, to date, been at all widely taken up in sociology, and insofar as sociology is to be understood as a population science, this situation would seem unlike to change in view of the fact that, in this context, the approach gives rise to at least three significant difficulties.

First of all, what is necessarily involved in pursuing the potential outcomes approach is – to take up an important distinction already found in the work of John Stuart Mill (1843/1973–74) – a focus on *the effects of causes* rather than on *the causes of effects*. Some putative cause of an outcome of interest is selected – whatever the motivation for this selection might be – and the aim is then to estimate its effect. This implies a very different orientation from starting out from effects, as, say, established population regularities, and then seeking a causal explanation of them. As already noted, the potential outcomes approach derives from, and has an apparent appropriateness in, applied research, including applied social research, where the effect of a given intervention is typically of prime interest: in other words, where the aim is to evaluate whether, or how far, some form of intervention – the cause – has achieved its objective in the sense of producing the effect that was sought.

However, the applicability of this approach to the central concerns of sociology as a population science would seem limited. Morgan and Winship (2007: 280) do in fact themselves acknowledge that if a researcher is primarily concerned with the causes of an observed effect, such as a demonstrated empirical regularity within a population, then the potential outcomes understanding of causation will be 'less helpful' (see also Gelman, 2011). And it is of further interest in this regard that, in a paper devoted to the treatment of causation in demography, as an established population science, Ní Bhrolcháin and Dyson (2007: 1–4) take the view that the 'interventionist' approach 'is not often applicable', because in demography 'the big questions are those about the causes of effects – what causes fertility change? what induces mortality decline?'.[7] And it might indeed be more generally maintained, following Popper (1972: 115), that 'In all sciences the ordinary approach is from the effects to the causes. The effect raises the problem – the problem to be explained... – and the scientist tries to solve it by constructing an explanatory hypothesis.'

Second, it has to be recognised that the potential outcomes approach does not escape from the criticism raised against attempts at demonstrating causation via regression that no account is provided of how the causal effect claimed is actually produced. Thus, Cox (1992: 297) would see it as a 'major limitation' of the approach that 'no explicit notion of an underlying process' is introduced 'at an observational level that is deeper than that involved in the data under immediate analysis'. And similar reservations would appear to underlie an increasing scepticism over recent years about whether *even in applied research* the potential outcomes approach – in particular as exemplified in RCTs – has necessarily to be taken as the 'gold standard' so far as causal inference is concerned.

An important social science example of such scepticism is provided by Deaton's (2010) discussion of methodologies for the evaluation of economic development assistance projects, as, say, in regard to poverty, health or education. Deaton is critical of the idea – as apparently now favoured by the World Bank – that RCTs should be given a

---

[7] Mahoney and Goertz (2006: 230–1) claim the 'causes of effects' orientation as a distinctive feature of qualitative sociology, in contrast to the 'effects of causes' orientation prevailing in quantitative sociology. This is, however, a quite groundless claim, and again illustrates the extremely limited – and self-serving – view of quantitative sociology (and political science) that proponents of logical methods of analysis characteristically take (see Achen's comment on Ragin in Chapter 4, n. 8). It may be added here that the approach to establishing the causes of effects in terms of INUS conditions (Mackie, 1974) that is favoured by Mahoney and Goertz comes up against exactly the same problems of moving from association to causation as occur in the case of regression. As Cartwright (2007: 34–5) puts it, '...INUS conditions are not causes. The INUS formula represents an association of features, a correlation, and we know that correlations may well be spurious'. For those unfamiliar with Mackie's work, an INUS condition is an *i*nsufficient but *n*ecessary part of an *u*nnecessary but *s*ufficient condition for some outcome to be realised. Of course, insofar as the social world, or at least our knowledge of it, has to be regarded as probabilistic, there are no necessary or sufficient causes anyway.

privileged position in such evaluation; and the main basis of his criticism is that, while RCTs may provide reliable information on *whether* particular projects succeeded, they can in themselves say little about *why*. In other words, they can say little about the 'underlying process', or the mechanisms, involved in success. It is, however, knowledge of these mechanisms, Deaton argues, that is crucial for determining the external validity of an RCT, or, that is, for determining how far a project that has been shown to 'work' in one population will work in another, perhaps quite different, population. For it is not the actual results of an RCT that can 'travel' – that can be generalised – from one such context to another, but only an understanding of the way in which these results were produced, and with then the requirement that due consideration be given to the conditions under which the mechanism in question is, or is not, likely to be maintained. (For further, more general and developed statements of essentially this position in regard to social policy formation and evaluation, see Pawson and Tilley, 1997; Cartwright and Hardie, 2012.)[8]

Third, where in sociology as a population science the attempt is made to give an account of the processes or mechanisms that create a causal relationship, this account is required, under the individualistic paradigm, to be one expressed ultimately in terms of individual action and interaction. However, this requirement then comes into direct conflict with Holland's maxim, basic to the potential outcomes approach, of 'no causation without manipulation'. This point is best

---

[8] Arguments running on much the same lines as Deaton's are also being advanced in the medical field in questioning whether clinical trials – often taken as the prime exemplars of the potential outcomes approach – should be viewed as setting the gold standard for evidence-based medicine (see e.g. Worrall, 2007; Steel, 2008; Thompson, 2011). Clinical trials do, however, tend to be more theoretically informed than RCTs carried out in the social field, and – as David Cox has pointed out to me – could often be regarded as attempts to further test ideas about mechanisms (see Chapter 9) that already have some empirical support, as, say, from laboratory work. A more appropriate extension of Deaton's argument would be to the predictions made from big data through entirely inductive, correlational analyses, where the concern is, quite explicitly, only with *what* and not with *why* (Mayer-Schönberger and Cukier, 2013: 4). Such predictions are, of course, heavily dependent on the future being like the past so far as underlying causal processes are concerned.

brought out by reference to the illuminating discussion that Holland himself provides of possible causal statements that are, and are not, compatible with this maxim. Holland (1986: 954–5) considers the following three statements (for present purposes, I have changed the order in which they appear in the original):

> She did well on the exam because she was coached by her teacher.
> She did well on the exam because she is a woman.
> She did well on the exam because she studied for it.

The first statement presents no problems from the standpoint of the potential outcomes approach: manipulation or an intervention – the coaching – occurred, and this can be taken as the cause of the woman doing well. With the second statement, some difficulty arises insofar as being a woman could be regarded as an 'intrinsic attribute' and thus one that is not open to manipulation. But, in sociology at least, it may often be possible to finesse such a difficulty by reinterpretation: for example, in the case in point, by taking 'because she is a woman' to refer not to unalterable biological sex but rather to socioculturally variable, and thus conceivably manipulable, gender. It is, however, the third statement that leads to a fundamental problem. This is so because, instead of there being any manipulation, the woman made what, to revert to the discussion of Chapter 3, could be regarded as an informed choice in pursuing a particular end: she wished to do well on the exam; she believed that studying for it was the best means to this end; she acted on this belief; and, her belief being correct, she did well.

As Holland observes, it is 'the voluntary aspect of the supposed cause' that here leads to incompatibility with the potential outcomes approach; and, he goes on, 'The voluntary nature of much of human activity makes causal statements about these activities difficult in many cases' (Holland, 1986: 955). But what, in effect, Holland has to be taken as saying here is 'difficult *given* the potential outcomes approach'. To which the response may be made that this in a further way indicates the limited relevance of this approach for sociology, or at all events for sociology understood as a population science. For, in this case, as has been maintained throughout, the ultimate aim is to give causal explanations of established population regularities in terms of social processes that are grounded in individual action – action in which a significant autonomous element, as expressed in informed choice and its implied rationality, has to be recognised.

An underlying issue here is a long-standing philosophical one of whether reasons can be causes. It was once fashionable to argue (see e.g., with specific reference to social science, Winch, 1958) that they could not be, since a cause has to be logically distinct from its effect and a reason is not logically distinct from the action to which it leads. But this view has subsequently lost favour to one in which individuals' reasons are seen as providing the basis for, perhaps a special, but still a quite legitimate form of causal explanation for their actions (see e.g. Davidson, 1980: ch. 1). It is, in effect, this latter view that I accept, and that I elaborate on in Chapter 9.

9 Causal explanation through social mechanisms

In order to provide causal explanations for established population regularities, causal processes, or mechanisms, must be hypothesized in terms of individual action and interaction that meet two requirements: they should be in principle adequate to generate the regularities in question and their actual operation should be open to empirical test. Advantage lies with mechanisms explicitly specified in terms of action that is in some sense rational.

Until well into the twentieth century, it was the standard view that causal explanations in science were arrived at by showing how observed phenomena followed from the operation of some general 'covering' law of a deterministic kind (see e.g. Hempel, 1965). And this view does indeed in various quarters persist.[1] However, with the probabilistic revolution, as discussed in Chapter 1, the idea of causal explanation as being dependent on the existence of deterministic laws was called into question, and in the more recent past a significantly different idea of the nature of such explanation has emerged and gained in acceptance. This is, in brief, the idea that causal explanations entail the spelling out, as fully as possible, of just *how* – through what continuous space–time processes or *mechanisms* – a supposed cause actually produces its effect (for extensive discussion from the standpoint of the philosophy of science, see Illari, Russo and Williamson, 2011).

Proponents of what could be called 'mechanism-based causal explanation' recognise that, from field to field, the nature of the

---

[1] For example, those who maintain from within sociology that it cannot become a science often attach great importance to its failure to produce general laws. But what is thus indicated is a limited understanding both of developments within the philosophy of science and of actual practice across the sciences – or, at all events, an undue preoccupation with classical physics. On the way in which the biological sciences offer far more instructive parallels for sociology as regards models of explanation, and more generally, see Lieberson and Lynn (2002).

mechanisms that will need to be envisaged and the ways in which they will be specified, in terms of the entities involved and their causal capacities, will vary widely. It may be recalled that Neyman – who can be regarded as an early adherent of the idea of mechanism-based explanation – emphasised that the mechanisms to be invoked in a population science in order to explain aggregate-level probabilistic regularities would be ones that, rather than being deterministic and applying to every individual case, themselves 'incorporated chance'. And in sociology understood as a population science, it would further seem clear that the key entities of such mechanisms must be individuals and that causal capacity must be taken to lie in the action of individuals and, ultimately, in the degree of autonomy that, through the possibility of informed choice, such action possesses (see Chapter 3). From this standpoint, then, the critiques previously noted of variable sociology in general and of regression analysis in particular for their neglect of the individual action underlying statistically established regularities can be taken to imply 'a plea for mechanisms' (Elster, 1998). What the movement in favour of mechanism-based explanation in sociology is essentially in search of is, in the words of Hedström and Bearman (2009a: 5), a means of 'making intelligible the regularities being observed by specifying in detail how they were brought about' – or, in other words, making these regularities not only visible but transparent.

It is important here to emphasise that seeking causal explanations in sociology in terms of mechanisms does not in itself entail some further advance of a technical kind. In particular, it is not a matter, as seems sometimes to be supposed, of simply including more possible 'intervening' variables within a statistical analysis or drawing more complex causal-path diagrams or graphs. The crucial input has to be a sociological and theoretical one. More specifically, what is needed and what, I would argue, sociologists seeking mechanism-based explanations have in fact generally aimed to provide, are what might be called *generalised narratives of action and interaction* that underlie regularities that call for explanation. To be of (potential) explanatory value, the mechanisms that are represented in these narratives need to possess two key features. First, they have to be (to use the term in a somewhat different sense to Max Weber) causally adequate: that is to say, it must be possible to show how, through individuals acting and interacting in the ways that are spelled out, the regularities of interest *could* be generated and sustained. Second, though, the narratives have to be ones expressed in such a form that the question of whether or not the mechanisms they specify *do in fact operate* in the way hypothesised is open to empirical examination, so that through further research the explanation offered can be either rejected or corroborated.

Some similarity may be seen between the formulation of narratives of the kind in question here and what proponents of qualitative case studies (e.g. Collier, Brady and Seawright, 2004; George and Bennett, 2005: ch. 7) refer to as 'causal process tracing' But, as Bennett (2008: 704) has acknowledged, insofar as this approach is applied to the explanation of singular events rather than of established regularities, what is involved is the spelling out of quite specific causal sequences – or, in other words, historical explanation (see Chapter 4) – rather than the identification of mechanisms that recurrently operate. As Elster (1998: 45–9) has observed, while explanations in terms of mechanisms have less generality than do explanations in terms of covering laws, they still aim to have greater generality than narratives of a quite idiographic kind.

In the development of mechanism-based explanations in sociology, two different approaches can be identified. Through distinguishing and comparing these approaches, certain issues of major importance can be brought out concerning the actual practice of constructing explanations in sociology as a population science.

One approach is that pursued most explicitly by Elster (1989, 2007), but which is also generally favoured by adherents of what has become known as 'analytical sociology' (Hedström and Swedberg, 1998b; Hedström and Bearman, 2009b). In this case, the aim could be seen as that of creating a kind of *catalogue raisonné* of mechanisms that operate in social life, ranging from the most elementary through to the most complex. What is then apparently envisaged is that sociologists confronted with an explanatory problem will be able to search this catalogue for mechanisms that would appear most likely to lead to a solution; or, to use the metaphor favoured by Elster (1989: 3) – and adopted by Hedström and Bearman – sociologists will be able to draw on the 'toolbox of mechanisms – nuts and bolts, cogs and wheels' that is made available.

The main advantage of this approach is that it opens up the possibility of theoretical integration and systematic development through the same or similar mechanisms being found to operate across a range of different substantive domains. And some success might in this regard be claimed – as, say, in the case of various social diffusion mechanisms, 'Matthew-effect' mechanisms of cumulative advantage and signalling mechanisms (for assessments, see Palloni, 1998, DiPrete and Eirich, 2006 and Gambetta, 2009, respectively).

However, the approach also has its dangers. Perhaps the most apparent is that it can give rise to a greater interest in mechanisms *per se* than in the extent of their explanatory potential: that is, beyond cases specially selected so as to best illustrate their application. Particular mechanisms and *what they might explain*, rather than established but non-transparent social regularities and *how they are to be explained*, become the foci of attention. In this way, then – and to return to the discussion of Chapter 8 – a concern becomes more evident with the effects of causes than with the causes of effects; or, one could say, attention centres simply on causal adequacy, in the sense previously indicated. However, as also indicated, while causal adequacy is necessary to a successful mechanism-based explanation, it is not sufficient. Evidence needs also to be provided that a hypothesised mechanism is that which does actually operate to produce the regularities that are under examination in any particular instance (Erikson, 1998).

A second approach to the development of mechanism-based explanations is then one which might be regarded as more congruent with the idea of sociology as a population science. This is the approach followed by sociologists whose starting point is with probabilistic population regularities that have been established in some substantive field of research but that remain without a satisfactory explanation: that is to say, they remain opaque rather than transparent regularities – the ways in which they derive from individual action and interaction, under the conditions of action that prevail, are not well understood. The question to be faced is therefore clearly one of the causes of effects.

This second approach, it has to be said, is not as developed as the first. As noted in Chapter 1, those sociologists who do focus their attention on population regularities have achieved far more in describing these regularities than in explaining them, or, that is, in making them visible rather than making them transparent. It has also to be recognised that, where causal mechanisms are hypothesised in relation to specific regularities, they may take on a somewhat *ad hoc* character. However, it is also likely that in such cases more than one mechanism can be envisaged, and in this way the importance is underlined of empirical testing designed to determine the relative merits of the differing explanations that are on offer.

It could thus be regarded as the most important feature of the second approach to mechanism-based explanation that, in pursuing it, one further quite crucial issue for sociology as a population science is brought to the fore: namely, that of *how – through what forms of research – one can best determine the actual operation of causal mechanisms*: or, that is, of social processes that lie, to revert to Cox's (1992: 297) phrase, at 'an observational level that is deeper than that involved in the data under immediate analysis'. As regards the methods of data collection and analysis they entail, these forms of research do not have to be the same as, and may in fact need to be different from, those that are essential in enabling population regularities – the explananda – to be reliably and accurately established.

To illustrate the problems – and the possibilities – that arise here, I consider attempts at explaining regularities that have become established in regard to inequalities of educational attainment among children of differing social backgrounds, and in particular of differing social class backgrounds. What has been shown through statistical analysis of survey data of various kinds is that these inequalities come about in two different ways, labelled as 'primary' and 'secondary' effects (Jackson, 2013). First, children from more advantaged class backgrounds on average perform better educationally than do children from less advantaged backgrounds: that is, in regard to grades, tests, examinations and so on; but, second, children from more advantaged backgrounds also tend to make more ambitious educational choices than do children from less advantaged backgrounds *even when level of previous performance is held constant.*

Advances in the understanding of primary effects have been made, and continue to be made, through the analysis of the complex interaction of sociocultural, economic and genetic influences at work; but secondary effects pose a different and also a more specifically sociological problem.[2] To seek to explain these effects simply by appealing to social class differences in values and norms relating to education is inadequate, since it is generally the case in modern societies that young people from all class backgrounds alike are steadily raising their levels of educational aspiration, participation and attainment, even while marked inequalities persist (see further Goldthorpe, 2007: vol. 2, chs 2–4). What is required is some narrative that, consistently with the individualistic paradigm, does not rely on unreflective and unconditional norm-following but takes account of individuals' ends, the constraints – non-normative as well as normative – under which they pursue these ends and the informed choices that they then make to pursue one course of action rather than another.

---

[2] In the case of primary effects, it is apparent that the causal mechanisms that operate are not only ones of sociological interest that can be expressed in terms, say, of the actions of parents relevant to their children's chances of educational success, as conditioned by the differing forms and levels of resources available to them, but also mechanisms that fall in the domains of epigenetics, neuroscience and developmental psychology.

RRA = Relative Risk Aversion Theory

A number of mechanisms on the lines in question have in fact been suggested. Certain authors (e.g. Esser, 1999; Becker, 2003) have adopted a rather standard 'expected utility' approach from micro-economics. Others, including Richard Breen and myself (Goldthorpe, 1996; Breen and Goldthorpe, 1997; cf. Erikson and Jonsson, 1996), have proposed mechanisms that are based on a more bounded and less demanding 'rationality of everyday life' (see Chapter 3). In what follows, I concentrate on what has become known as the Breen–Goldthorpe 'relative risk aversion' (RRA) theory, not so as to privilege my own work but simply because my concern is with how mechanism-based explanations in sociology are to be evaluated through further research and because the RRA theory has in fact been subject to far more, and more varied, empirical testing than others in the field.[3]

The basic claim of the RRA theory is that, when making educational choices with their futures in mind, young people, and their parents, will give priority to the avoidance of downward social mobility over the achievement of upward mobility.[4] However, while risk aversion can then be seen as equal, relative to social origins, *the actual risks involved* in educational choice will be unequal. For children of

---

[3] In Goldthorpe (2007: vol. 2, ch. 4), I review results from six different tests, and others could have been included: Holm and Jaeger (2008) refer to four further tests prior to making one of their own (see subsequent text), and I am aware of several others of still more recent date. I previously concluded that, although various difficulties with the RRA theory had been revealed and the need for refinements and further development indicated, it remains, in its essentials, 'alive'. And this is the position I would still adhere to. Interesting attempts at taking the theory further can be found in Breen and Yaish (2006) and Breen, van de Werfhorst and Jaeger (2014). I have myself (Goldthorpe, 2007: vol. 2, ch. 7) attempted to extend the theory to intergenerational class mobility and hope to continue this work in the light of further empirical research into social mobility in which I am currently involved.

[4] The theory could then be regarded as a special case of the more general 'prospect theory' propounded by Kahneman and Tversky (1979), according to which the slope of individuals' utility curves is steeper in the domain of losses than in the domain of gains. However, I would not myself wish to follow Kahneman (2011: 286) in supposing that a 'failure of rationality' is 'built into prospect theory' – or, therefore, into the RRA theory – simply because it violates the logic of choice inherent in expected utility theory (see Chapter 3, n. 7).

more advantaged social origins, there will be little to lose, in seeking to maintain their parents' position, by taking up all further educational opportunities that their previous performance makes available to them – and even if their chances of ultimate success may be doubtful. But for children of less advantaged social origins, educational choice will be more problematic. For, in their case, more ambitious choices that might end in failure could not only be in various ways costly in themselves but could also preclude less ambitious choices that, even if not offering great prospects for advancement, would at all events still effectively guard against downward mobility. Consequently, for these children to make a more ambitious choice, they would need to have a greater assurance of success – as would be indicated by a higher level of previous performance – than would their more advantaged counterparts.

If the mechanism spelled out by such a narrative were in operation then secondary effects in class inequalities in educational attainment would be generated through rather straightforward aggregation. The mechanism could, in other words, be regarded as causally adequate. But how can it be determined whether, or how far, it is in fact at work? At least three different research strategies can in this regard be identified – each, of course, requiring that, to revert to the argument of Chapter 5, relevant variables should be conceptualised and made operational in appropriate ways.

The first strategy could be described as that of direct observation. If causal mechanisms are understood as continuous space–time processes, then it should, in principle, be possible to obtain direct evidence of their operation wherever this is going on, and intensive, appropriately focused case studies could thus be of value (see pp. 78–9). As regards the RRA theory a good deal of research has in fact been aimed at testing its consistency with results obtained from detailed interviews with samples of young people (e.g. Need and de Jong, 2000; Sullivan, 2006) or with their parents (e.g. Stocké, 2007) that focus on educational goals, plans and expectations. It has in this way been found *inter alia* that, while general attitudes towards education and its intrinsic and extrinsic value differ little by class background, eventual educational choices are often, if not invariably, influenced by considerations of maintaining parental levels of both education and social class – as would be expected under the theory. At the same time, though, it has also been indicated through such research that there are other factors that may additionally serve to create secondary effects: for example, a tendency for students' assessments of their own ability to be higher the more advantaged their social backgrounds, even when previous performance is controlled, and also a tendency for informational as well as economic constraints to be greater for students from less advantaged backgrounds.

The second research strategy involves what could, in contrast, be described as attempts at the indirect observation of hypothesised causal mechanisms. In this case, the aim is to show that the mechanism under examination implies *other* regularities apart from those that it is intended to explain, and then to see if these regularities can be demonstrated.[5] With the RRA theory, a particularly good example of this strategy is provided by the work of Davies, Heinesen and Holm (2002) and Holm and Jaeger (2008). What these authors note is that under the RRA theory, the effect of parental background on children's educational choices should not be continuous throughout their educational careers but rather 'kinked', in that it should weaken once children have reached an educational level that gives them a high probability of avoiding downward mobility. Through analyses of data on students' transitions within the Danish educational system, it is then shown that these derived expectations from the RRA theory are to a large extent, even if not always, supported.

The third possible research strategy is experimental rather than observational. It may be that in the light of a proposed causal

---

[5] This strategy can be seen as entailing the 'hypothetico-deductive' method as classically proposed by Popper (1959). At the same time, though, it is dependent on other regularities being derivable from the theory under examination – which in turn lends force to what has become known as the 'Fisher dictum'. Cochran (1965) reports that when R. A. Fisher was asked how observational studies could best be made to yield causal conclusions, he replied, 'Make your theories elaborate': that is, potentially exposed to testing in as many different ways as possible.

mechanism, an experimental, or at least quasi-experimental, study can be designed, through which it can be assessed how far an intervention or 'treatment' (see the discussion of Chapter 8) has effects of the kind that would be expected if the mechanism were in fact in operation. That is to say, in this context an 'effects of causes' approach may appropriately be taken up (see Gelman and Imbens, 2013). As regards the RRA theory, no specific experimental test has so far been developed. However, a major study approximating an RCT in its design, and influenced in part by the RRA theory, is presently under way in Italy.[6] The effects are being investigated of providing students in a sample of secondary schools with specialist advice on their chances of success if they go on to university (given their academic performance to date), on the costs they are likely to incur in taking up particular courses and on the returns they are likely to gain. By then comparing the choices made by students who received this advice with those in a control sample of schools who received no advice, it will be possible to make some estimate of the importance of purely informational as distinct from economic constraints on the decision to enter higher education. Under the RRA theory, the expectation would be that, while some reduction in secondary effects in class inequalities may in this way be achieved, such effects will largely remain, since differences in the risks involved in this decision related to class inequalities in economic resources will still be in operation.

These different research strategies that may be followed in testing hypothesised causal mechanisms are not to be ranked in some order of importance. Each has its own advantages and disadvantages. What is important is that the actual operation of mechanisms should be tested in as many ways as is possible and the results obtained be considered in relation to one another.[7] It should not be expected that

---

[6] The study is directed by Professor Antonio Schizzerotto at the Research Institute for the Evaluation of Public Policy, Trento.

[7] One other possible strategy is that conducted via what has become known as agent-based computational (ABC) modelling. In this case (see Epstein, 2006: ch. 1), the basic idea would be to ask how a given population regularity could be generated through the actions and interactions of heterogeneous and autonomous agents, and then to

any particular test will produce 'clinching' results, at least not of a positive kind, but at best 'vouching' results – to take up Cartwright's (2007: ch. 3) useful distinction; and greatest weight has then to be given to how far results from different tests do or do not 'fit together'. In this regard, Haack's (1998: ch. 5 'crossword-puzzle model' for the evaluation of evidence in relation to a hypothesis, emphasising the consistency or inconsistency of the implications of different empirical findings, would appear especially apt (see also Cox and Donnelly, 2011: chs 1, 2).[8]

The approach to mechanism-based explanations in sociology that starts out from some established population regularity as the explanandum does then tend to differ from the approach aiming to create a catalogue, or toolbox, of explanatory mechanisms in the importance that is attached to the question of whether a mechanism is that which is actually in operation in a particular instance – over and above the question of its causal adequacy. There is, moreover, one other difference that emerges between the two approaches that is of some consequence and that should in conclusion also be noted.

With the catalogue approach, a quite catholic view is taken – appropriately enough – as regards the theoretical basis of the mechanisms that are specified. Thus, Hedström and Bearman (2009a: 22, n. 1) point out that, although proponents of mechanism-based explanation in sociology do in general seek to specify mechanisms in terms

---

attempt to construct a model that could be shown, through computer simulation, to be capable of 'growing' the regularity in question. This strategy can provide a strong test of the causal adequacy – or of what ABC modellers refer to as the 'generative sufficiency' – of a proposed mechanism, and interesting and theoretically suggestive applications are now emerging in both sociology and demography (see e.g. Todd, Billari and Simão, 2005 for a model able to reproduce observed regularities in age at first marriage, based on 'fast and frugal' heuristics). However, to repeat the point made in the text, to show the generative sufficiency of a mechanism is not to show that it is in fact this mechanism that is in some particular instance at work.

[8] I am grateful to Jan Vandenbroucke for drawing my attention to Haack's work and also (together with David Cox) to a classic paper in epidemiology that provides an outstanding illustration of the crossword-puzzle model in application: the meta-analysis of the evidence for smoking as a cause of lung cancer by Cornfield et al. (1959).

of the action and interaction of individuals, this does not imply a similarly general commitment to rational-action theory. The mechanisms proposed as the 'nuts and bolts, cogs and wheels' of sociological explanations may be ones in which key importance attaches to action that is primarily orientated to the expectations of others and to conformity with the social norms that prevail within groups, social networks, communities and so on. However, insofar as sociologists concerned with population regularities of a well-established but still opaque kind have sought mechanism-based explanations of these regularities, the tendency has been for these mechanisms to be envisaged as entailing action that could indeed be understood as rational – albeit more often, as with the RRA theory, in a bounded rather than in a demonic sense. — lol

The significance of this difference does then emerge in regard to what is perhaps the strongest objection that has thus far been put forward to the idea of mechanism-based explanation, both in general and in the social sciences in particular. This is the objection (see e.g. Kincaid, 2011; cf. King, Keohane and Verba, 1994: ch. 3) that seeking the generative mechanisms that underlie observed regularities leads in effect to an infinite regress. The philosopher Patrick Suppes observed some time ago that '. . . the mechanisms postulated and used by one generation are mechanisms that are to be explained and understood themselves in terms of more primitive mechanisms by the next generation' – or, in short, that 'one man's mechanism is another man's black box' (Suppes, 1970: 91). And the question can then be raised of whether in this process there is any evident stopping point – except perhaps through some appeal to 'covering laws' of nature (themselves inexplicable) of the kind that mechanism-based explanation is aimed at avoiding.

With regard to the social sciences, Hedström (2005: 27–8) has argued that appropriate stopping points can be identified: that is, where the mechanisms invoked are no longer ones that lie within the range of interest of these disciplines, but, presumably ones which extend into the biological or physical sciences. But a stronger response is in fact possible. Insofar as mechanisms that are taken to explain population regularities appeal to action reflecting social norms, then, even if it can be shown that these mechanisms are indeed in operation, further questions remain open and need to be pursued: that is, as previously argued in Chapter 3, questions of why it is *these* norms rather than others that are influential and of why individuals do conform with these norms rather than contravening or perhaps openly challenging them. Until questions of this kind are answered, it could be held that black boxes clearly do exist. In contrast, insofar as the action involved in a mechanism can be treated as rational – even if only in a subjective, bounded sense of being seen by the individuals concerned as that best suited to attaining their ends, given the conditions under which they are required to act – a different situation obtains. In this case, a stopping point could be thought to have been reached in that, as Hollis (1977: 21; cf. Boudon, 2003a, Introduction) has put it, 'rational action is its own explanation'; or, as argued by Coleman (1986: 1), the rational action of individuals, even if the rationality is only subjective, is 'understandable' action that we need ask no more questions about and thus has 'a unique attractiveness' as the basis of sociological theory. In other words, if the 'bottom line' of a sociological explanation is not social norms but rather rational action – which may or may not result in conformity with norms – both explanatory *and* hermeneutic requirements are in this way met (see further Goldthorpe, 2007: vol. 1, ch. 7).[9]

---

[9] Watts has argued that explanations of social phenomena in terms of what he calls 'rationalizable action', while attractive in providing 'understandability', still 'cannot in general be expected to satisfy the standards of causal explanation' (Watts, 2014: 314–15). However, the standards he supposes are those of the potential outcomes approach, which, as maintained in the previous chapter, can be questioned at least as regards their applicability in sociology; and further, as his paper goes on, it appears to turn essentially into a plea for the testing of explanatory models that invoke 'rationalizable action' on an out-of-sample basis – that is, on the basis of data and analyses other than those which led to their initial formulation – which is of course entirely in line with the argument of this chapter. Further questions could of course be raised concerning the ends towards which rational action is directed. However, as observed in Chapter 2, how far individuals' choice of ends is open to systematic explanation of any kind remains a matter of serious doubt.

In the context of sociology as a population science, the search for mechanism-based explanations of established probabilistic regularities could then be said to proceed with two distinctive emphases. First, and consistently with a concern for the causes of effects, the emphasis is less on the effects that mechanisms *could* produce than on the testing of whether proposed mechanisms are those actually at work in particular cases of interest. Second, and consistently with the underlying individualistic paradigm, the emphasis is on mechanisms that can be ultimately expressed in terms of individuals' informed choices among the possibilities that they see as open to them and of the rationality involved in such choices and the action that follows from them.

[handwritten margin notes: Testing & Explanatory Various Mechanisms / Based on Theories of Social action]

Conclusion

In this concluding chapter, I do not aim to summarise what has gone before. I noted in the Introduction that readers wanting an overview of the argument of the book could simply read through the propositions with which the central chapters are headed. I hope that those who at this stage feel in need of some recapitulation might find it sufficient to do likewise. What I wish to consider here is *what might be thought to follow* if my case for an understanding of sociology as a population science were to be accepted. More specifically, I am concerned with the implications for sociology itself as an academic discipline, for its relations with other disciplines and for its public role.

For sociology as a discipline, what would perhaps most obviously follow insofar as it became understood as a population science is that the scope to which it presently pretends would be significantly reduced. That is to say, in taking population regularities as its proper explananda, in focusing on establishing the extent and form of such regularities through statistically grounded methods and on developing and testing mechanism-based explanations of their generation and persistence, there is no question that sociology would address a narrower range of topics, through less diverse research styles and with a more limited conception of its ultimate goals than is presently the case. Abbott (2001: 5–6) has observed that sociology 'is not very good at excluding things from itself' and that 'once an area makes a claim for sociological attention, the discipline doesn't have any *intellectually* effective way of denying that claim' (emphasis in original). Sociology as a population science would have such a way, that is, in being based on a relatively clear definition of what are, and are not, its appropriate objects of study – and of what are in turn its appropriate methods of data collection and analysis and modes of explanation.

From this point of view, to echo Mies van der Rohe, less would be more.

However, it is, I recognise, on the grounds that it would imply a clear diminution of the extent and diversity of the sociological domain that the idea of sociology as a population science is most likely to be disputed and resisted. In anticipation of such a reaction, I might then restate a point that I already emphasised in the Introduction. My concern in arguing for sociology as a population science is not so much with advancing a normative programme – that is, with telling sociologists what they should do – as with setting out a more considered rationale for the way in which a large and increasing number of them appear in fact already to practise sociology, and with helping in this way to provide the basis on which, in my view, the development of a scientific sociology could best proceed. The counter-arguments to my position that I would therefore take as being of main relevance and weight, as again I stressed in the Introduction, would be ones put forward by sociologists who have a commitment to this same project but who would see other routes ahead as being more promising. And responses made on such lines – responses indicating alternative models for sociology as a science – I would regard as representing a very positive outcome of the present work. As for those sociologists who would favour quite different agendas – as, say, for some form of 'humanistic' or sociopolitically 'committed' sociology – they will no doubt still seek to carry through their own projects, and it could thus be expected that the highly pluralistic character of sociology, considered overall, will in fact be maintained.

In this connection, though, two further points might be made. The first is the rather obvious one that there is a stage when pluralism within a discipline becomes a liability rather than an asset: that is, when the existence of disciplinarity has itself to be called into question. For example, as a British sociologist, but one working chiefly within a European context, I have to observe that in the light of an examination, on the one hand, of the majority of papers appearing in such British journals as *Sociology* or the *Sociological Review* and, on the other, of the majority of those appearing in the *European Sociological Review* or *Acta Sociologica* (edited from the Nordic countries), it would be no easy task to explain in just what sense these could be said to reflect work in one and the same discipline. This cannot be a favourable circumstance as regards either the standing of sociology within academia or its chances of maintaining public support, moral or material.[1] Furthermore, at least for those seeking to develop sociology as a science, pluralism must always stand in some tension with the aim of achieving what Ziman (1968) has referred to as 'consensible' knowledge. While on the frontiers of research, divergent and conflicting views, debate and controversy are to be expected and indeed play a crucial role in the scientific process, at some stage frontier disputes have to translate into the growth of 'core' knowledge on which all competent workers in the field can agree. Insofar as this does not happen in sociology, claims that it might make to scientific status are clearly undermined (Cole, 1994).

The second, and related, point is then that within the pluralism of present-day sociology, those whose concern is primarily with its development as a science can legitimately assert, and exploit, a right to criticise, on what they would regard as scientific grounds, work emerging from versions of sociology directed towards other goals: that is, on grounds ultimately of the quality of the data and the data analysis involved and the logical consistency of evidence and argument.

---

[1] It might, however, be thought that the European situation has more potential for development than that existing in the US: that is, insofar as differences in conceptions of sociology and in its actual practice are becoming more structured *among* university departments and research centres, professional associations and even countries. Thus, possibilities would appear to exist for at least some *de facto* reorganisation, allowing those who wish to pursue sociology as a social science to go their own way. In the US, in contrast, pluralism – or, one might say, fragmentation – would appear more strongly embedded *within* universities and associations. In particular, the American Sociological Association, viewed from outside, does appear as something of a whited sepulchre, having all the paraphernalia of a professional association serving an academic discipline while revealing a serious lack of internal consensus over what the essentials of this discipline are. By way of illustration, see the debate over 'public sociology' as conducted in, for example, Clawson et al. (2007), and taken up later in the text.

In other words, those who reject the idea of sociology as a science cannot, through such a rejection, create some kind of immunity for themselves against challenges to their own knowledge claims. This is a matter that I pursue further in regard to the public role of sociology discussed later in this chapter.

Next, however, I turn to the implications of understanding sociology as a population science for its relations with other academic disciplines, and the reorientation of sociology that I would envisage is, I accept, again likely to be a cause of dissension.

Most disturbingly for some will no doubt be what appears to follow for the relationship between sociology and history. The argument of Chapter 4 in particular clearly entails a rejection of the idea advanced by authors such as Giddens (1979) and Abrams (1980) that no significant borderline between sociology and history as academic disciplines need in fact be recognised. What I maintain here is that the historical mode of explanation as applied in the case of singular events, or complexes of such events, is clearly different from the sociological mode as applied in the case of demonstrated regularities in events. Historical explanations, while perhaps drawing on theory from various sources, remain time- and place-specific narratives of action and interaction in which an important role has almost always to be given to sheer contingency – to essential chance. Sociological explanations aim to be narratives as generalised in time and place as possible, and while the causal mechanisms or processes to which they refer will incorporate chance, this is a chance that is 'tamable', in that explananda and explanations alike are of a probabilistic character.[2]

To avoid any misunderstanding, I would at the same time emphasise that the idea of sociology as a population science in no way precludes or is inimical to research undertaken *in the context of historical societies*. To the contrary, insofar as it is possible to

---

[2] I have elsewhere (Goldthorpe, 2007: vol. 1, ch. 2) sought also to show basic methodological differences between history and sociology in regard to the kinds of data on which they are able to draw, and to bring out some of the implications of these differences.

obtain appropriate data, the investigation of population regularities in such societies can be of major value. I noted in Chapter 2 that research of the kind in question – whether carried out as 'historical sociology' or as 'social science history' – has played an important role in undermining naïve notions of 'traditional' societies and communities deriving from the holistic paradigm. And work in a similar vein is now contributing substantially to our understanding of both commonalities and variation across early modern and industrialising societies in such areas as family formation, household structure, the occupational division of labour and social stratification and mobility. I would see work produced by, for example, the Cambridge Group for the History of Population and Social Structure or the Historical International Social Mobility Analysis (HISMA) network, centred at the University of Utrecht, as indeed providing notable illustrations of sociology as a population science.

While the relationship between sociology and history is then one that would call for some clearer differentiation if sociology were to be understood as a population science, other instances do at the same time arise where such an understanding would in fact weaken disciplinary boundaries, if not effectively remove them. This is most clearly the case with sociology and demography – an already established population science.

In the middle decades of the twentieth century, especially in countries such as the US and Britain, and also France, the two disciplines were in fact already close. Researchers, whether nominally sociologists or demographers, treated similar issues and used essentially similar methodologies – as, for example, in such fields as the determinants of fertility, homogamy and heterogamy, migration patterns, residential segregation by ethnicity or social status, educational inequalities and social mobility. But, subsequently, some greater distancing became apparent. On the side of sociology, this would seem to have been mainly the result of the 'reaction against positivism': that is, against quantitative research in general. On the side of demography, fears arose that a focus on micro-level social processes meant that the discipline was 'abandoning its core' (Lee, 2001): that is, the study of human populations at the macro-level on the basis primarily of census and registration data, rather than survey data, and through established measurement procedures and formal models.

However, what would now appear to be emerging within demography is a recognition that little conflict is in fact here involved – and with a consequent reopening of opportunities for, in effect, disciplinary integration with sociology under the auspices of population science. As Billari (2015) has argued (see also Xie, 2000), the first stage of demographic inquiry can indeed be taken as that of the description – often the highly sophisticated description – of regularities in population movements over place and time; but a second stage naturally follows of seeking for explanations of these regularities in terms of causal processes or mechanisms operating at the micro-level of individual action and interaction. The parallels with an understanding of sociology on the lines for which I have argued are evident enough. While demography viewed in the way that Billari proposes has itself to be an interdisciplinary subject – the causal processes invoked in the second stage may be ones involving, say, biology or psychology as well as sociology – the linkages with sociology could be expected to be of central importance.

A further, rather less obvious case where the shared idea of population science could make for greater and potentially highly rewarding collaboration arises with sociology and epidemiology. Here also, a relatively close interdisciplinary relationship in the mid-twentieth century tended later to weaken.[3] In sociology, the focus changed from 'sociology in medicine' to 'the sociology of medicine', with associated criticism of the 'medical model' of illness and treatment, which

---

[3] This close relationship was especially apparent in Britain. Some of the most impressive seminars and conferences that I attended as a young sociologist were ones in which epidemiologists of the calibre of Jerry Morris and Abe Adelstein came together with medical sociologists such as Raymond Illsley and others from his Medical Research Council centre in Aberdeen and social policy specialists such as Richard Titmuss and Brian Abel-Smith.

had the effect of alienating many medical researchers (in my view, quite understandably so). At the same time, in epidemiology, a growing emphasis came to be placed on the empirical determination of individual-level risk factors for diseases, with often only a limited interest being shown either in the population distributions of diseases or in the causal mechanisms underlying risks.

Again, though, promising counter-tendencies would now appear to be in train. In epidemiology, a reaction against the dominance of 'risk-factor' and 'black-box' approaches and a renewed insistence on epidemiology as a population science can both be traced from the later 1990s (see e.g. Susser, 1998; Pearce, 1999, 2011). The importance is stressed of retaining, on the one hand, a concern with the description and analysis of disease distributions, since in this way hitherto unrecognised public health problems can often be revealed – or, that is, new epidemiological explananda created – and, on the other hand, a concern with underlying causal processes operating at all levels from the molecular to the societal. In this latter respect, then, significant opportunities are opened up for collaboration between the now increasing numbers of self-identified 'social epidemiologists' (Galea and Link, 2013) and those sociologists who, moving on from medical sociology, now work in the more widely conceived field of the sociology of health and illness, with a population orientation providing the common ground.

One can, I believe, realistically envisage the development in the years ahead of research centres in the human population sciences in which sociologists, demographers and social epidemiologists would be brought together and in which research would be pursued on such lines that disciplinary boundaries would be in large part transcended.

There is one other academic relationship that rather obviously calls for attention here: that between sociology and economics. How would this be affected by the understanding of sociology as a population science? In certain respects, it might be thought that in this way sociology and economics would be brought somewhat closer together: that is, through the adoption in sociology of the individualistic paradigm – of methodological individualism – to which economics has always been committed, and further through the privileging, from both explanatory and hermeneutic standpoints, of individual action that can be treated as in some sense rational. However, major divergences are still in fact to be expected.

First of all, on the side of economics the consequences persist of what has been described (Bruni and Sugden, 2007) as 'the Pareto turn' at the beginning of the twentieth century, as a result of which economics sought explicitly to establish itself as a 'separate science' from psychology and sociology: that is, as one founded on theory derived deductively from axioms of rational choice that claimed objective correctness and that were in no way dependent on research into how individuals actually did make choices and act upon them. In contrast, on the side of sociology the rejection of the holistic and the acceptance of the individualistic paradigm of inquiry have been associated with a concern for as realistic an understanding as possible of the psychological and social processes involved in individual choice and in turn, so far as rationality is concerned, with a refusal of demonic in favour of bounded conceptions. Moreover, it is by no means clear that the more recent development of behavioural economics has done much to bridge the gap. Aside from having doubts about the external validity of much of the experimental work being undertaken, sociologists might also wish to question the degree of commitment to empirical realism: that is, whether all that is involved is the creation of more complicated utility functions through the inclusion of 'social' preferences (see e.g. Rabin, 1998), while little interest is shown in the way in which decision-making in everyday social life is actually carried through (see Berg and Gigerenzer, 2010).

Second, and relatedly, the approach to questions of the 'fit' between theory and the results of empirical research would appear very different as between at least mainstream economics and sociology practised as a population science. Economists dealing with some substantive issue tend to regard this as primarily a matter of applying deductively derived theory and then treat empirical findings as serving to illustrate, or further, perhaps, to quantify, the theory. The idea that such findings could serve to *test* theory and might therefore lead to its rejection – implying a falsificationist methodological approach – has never found much favour among those committed to the idea of economics as a separate science (Blaug, 1992; Hausman, 1992). *In extremis*, resort can always be made to the argument that, since the theory embodies objectively correct principles of choice, any deviation from it indicates that it is the actors involved who are 'wrong' – that is, who display ignorance or error – rather than the theory itself. In contrast, sociology as a population science would begin with establishing empirically the regularities that constitute the explananda in some area of substantive interest and then seek for mechanism-based explanations, which, while quite possibly lacking the degree of theoretical coherence found in economics, would always have to be open to evaluation, positive or negative, in the light of further research.

Insofar as there are any indications of disciplinary convergence, they stem from the development – exciting but still minoritarian – of what has become known as the 'new economics thinking', and especially as this focuses on a more empirical approach to the analysis of economic issues.[4] As perhaps the most notable examples of work in this vein, one could cite the studies of economic inequality, based on extensive research into the distributions of income and wealth and their variation over place and change over time, that have been carried out by economists such as Tony Atkinson, Thomas Piketty and their associates (see esp. Atkinson, 2008; Atkinson and Piketty, 2010; Piketty, 2014). What is emphasised in these studies, and is clearly suggestive of a population approach, is the importance – to draw on Piketty (2014: 3, 20, 31–2) – first of all of determining through detailed statistical research and analysis relevant 'facts and patterns'

---

[4] The two leading centres in this connection are the Institute for New Economic Thinking in New York and the Institute for New Economic Thinking at the Oxford University Martin School.

concerning inequality, instead of producing 'purely theoretical results without even knowing what facts needed to be explained'; and then, having established the specific explananda, of hypothesising at the level of individual action 'economic, social, and political mechanisms that might explain them', and with the obvious implication that 'economics should never have sought to divorce itself from the other social sciences and can advance only in conjunction with them'.

Finally, I come to the implications of the idea of sociology as a population science for its public role. In recent years, discussion of the role that sociology might play outside of academia has largely turned on the idea of 'public sociology', as advanced by Michael Burawoy in his 2004 Presidential Address to the American Sociological Association (Burawoy, 2005). I can then take this idea as a convenient point of reference, and all the more so since the position for which I would argue stands in more or less direct opposition to that of Burawoy.

As regards the extra-academic significance of sociology, it is crucial for Burawoy to make a distinction between what he refers to as 'policy sociology' and the 'public sociology' that he aims to promote. Policy sociology, Burawoy claims, is 'sociology in the service of a goal defined by a client'; its *raison d'être* is to provide solutions to predefined problems or to legitimate supposed solutions already in place. In contrast, public sociology, especially in its 'organic' rather than 'traditional' forms, involves 'a dialogic relation' between sociologists and a variety of publics over issues of shared political and moral concern in which a mutual adjustment of interests and values is sought, with the possibility of action towards common ends then being pursued (Burawoy, 2005: 9).

From the standpoint of sociology as a population science, the distinction here set up has little merit. While Burawoy's conception of public sociology envisages a significantly larger role for sociology, as a social science, than it can in fact legitimately seek to fulfil, his conception of policy sociology is, on the other hand, quite unnecessarily restricted. At the heart of the matter is a further, and yet more questionable, distinction that Burawoy wishes to make:

that between 'instrumental' and 'reflexive' knowledge. Instrumental knowledge, according to Burawoy, is the knowledge that derives from the professional practice of sociology, and that may be applied in policy sociology. In contrast, reflexive knowledge is said to result from the dialogues of public sociology and is knowledge concerned not with means but with the ultimate ends of society (Burawoy, 2005: 11). However, what Burawoy then quite fails to explain is just *how* such reflexive knowledge is obtained, tested and codified, let alone *why* – on what grounds – he supposes that the ends of society can in any event *be* an object of knowledge as opposed to a matter of value choice – choice that sociology in fact best serves to clarify and to sharpen.[5]

In response, what has then to be insisted on is that, while sociologists are of course as free as other citizens to engage in sociopolitical action, there is no reason to accept that through such engagement they gain access to some special kind of knowledge. Any knowledge supposedly emergent from public sociology, as Burawoy would understand it, must stand exposed to exactly the same critical examination as that which derives from professional sociology. In other words, reflexive knowledge – whatever it is supposed to mean – cannot be knowledge that has a privileged status simply in respect of the sociopolitical values that it is taken to underwrite. And, as commentators on Burawoy have observed (e.g. Turner, 2007), many of the works he cites as prime examples of public sociology have in fact been far more successful in attracting public attention than in convincing other sociologists of their soundness. Neither 'commitment' nor 'impact' provides any guarantee of scientific quality; and sociologists should be ready to recognise that this is so just as much in the

---

[5] Burawoy at one point states that 'Public sociology has no intrinsic normative valence' (Burawoy, 2005: 8). But he also argues that since sociology owes its existence to 'civil society', sociologists have an obligation to commit to the values of civil society (Burawoy, 2004). The difficulty then is that these values are spelled out in ways either that are so general as to beg all crucial questions or that some sociologists could quite reasonably wish to dispute. Note Nielsen's (2004) pertinent observations on 'the vacant we' in Burawoy's public sociology.

case of work which appears to reflect their own value positions as in that which does not.

While, then, Burawoy's public sociology, based on reflexive knowledge, pretends to a role that any sociology with claims to scientific status cannot – and should not attempt to – fulfil, it is difficult to see his conception of policy sociology, based on instrumental knowledge, as being other than a deliberately impoverished one. The idea that policy sociology can operate only in the service of a goal defined by a client or so as to legitimate existing policies is far removed from reality. Many sociologists in fact enter the policy field in order to argue that policies, whether those of governments or of other agencies, are misconceived and thus likely to fail in attaining their objectives or to have damaging side-effects; or, yet more radically, to argue that the problems towards which policies are directed have been inadequately understood. And in these respects, sociology as a population science can have particular force, since it is very often the form of population regularities and the social processes through which they are generated and sustained that is centrally at issue.

For example, in Britain since the 1990s, as now more recently in the US, social mobility has become a major political concern. But, in Britain at least, most related discussion of policy has been predicated on the view that social mobility is in decline, even though survey research indicates in most respects a rather remarkable degree of stability (see e.g. Bukodi et al., 2014); and at the same time, the difficulty experienced by politicians and their policy advisors in grasping the standard sociological distinction between absolute and relative mobility rates (see p. 15) has led to deep confusion over what would be entailed in increasing mobility and over what policies would and would not have some chance of success. If I (Goldthorpe, 2013) and others have attempted to bring these points out, why should this not be regarded as policy sociology?

Or, as a further example, one could take the concern apparent in family policy in many countries over the possibly negative effects on children – on, say, their emotional development or educational progress – of rising rates of parental break-up. In this case, too, much confusion has arisen in regard to what negative effects are and are not securely established, and further, and more seriously, in regard to the causal processes involved. Policy has often been based on the assumption that it is break-up itself that is the key causal factor and has therefore been aimed at reducing its frequency. But this position has been called into question by sociologists and demographers (for a valuable review, see Ní Bhrolcháin, 2001), who have pointed to evidence that other variables may lie behind *both* break-up and adverse outcomes for children – most obviously, although not only, parental conflict – and with then the implication that fewer break-ups need not have the positive consequences hoped for and that in some cases break-up may in fact be the least damaging option. Again, why is this not to be regarded as a case of policy sociology in action?

In sum, sociology as a population science could appropriately and effectively fulfil a public role in providing the grounding for a policy sociology far less passive and uncritical than that characterised by Burawoy, while at the same time making no claims to give access to special – or, one might well say, spurious – forms of knowledge that can determine what the ultimate ends of a society should be.[6]

Max Weber (1921/1948, 1922/1948), in his two magnificent essays on 'Politics as a Vocation' and 'Science as a Vocation', saw a major extra-academic objective of science as being 'to gain *clarity*' as to its public role (1922/1948: 151, emphasis in original): that is, clarity as to what are those issues on which science can properly speak – issues of fact, analysis and theory; and what are those that lie beyond its limits – issues arising in 'the various value spheres of the world [that] stand in irreconcilable conflict with each other' (1922/48:

---

[6] Rather remarkably, Burawoy (2005: 23) appears to accept that sociology cannot compete with economics in 'the policy world' – in part because of the greater intellectual coherence that economics possesses – and should not in fact attempt to do so. I would regard this as quite misguided and sadly defeatist. Sociology should always be ready to compete with economics in exerting influence on policy issues – aggressively so, if need be. And, at least if understood as a population science, it has the capacity do so to very good effect.

147). As Weber well appreciated, the two kinds of issue do inevitably interconnect, and especially so in the social domain, for example, in regard to the extent to which particular values can, under given conditions, be realised; through what forms of policy and indeed polity; and with what further, unintended and possibly unwanted, consequences. And he also observed that there is an ever-present tendency for political actors to seek to show that the facts, analysis and theory are 'on their side', and often to resort to selectivity, distortion or downright misrepresentation in order to strengthen their case. This tendency in itself Weber could actually view with some detachment, since he appreciated that embracing politics as a vocation did entail accepting that means might have to be justified in terms of ends. He reserved his most scathing criticism not for political actors who tried to exploit science but rather for those individuals who tried to exploit their scientific positions and authority in order to give some privileged status to what were no more than their own sociopolitical preferences. And, in turn, he insisted that those for whom science was truly a vocation – those who had a primary value-commitment to science – should always assume responsibility for maintaining the necessary clarity over the knowledge claims that science could and could not legitimately make, and should at the same time always be ready to face up to scientific findings that were, from their own extra-scientific standpoints, 'inconvenient' (1922/1948: 145–50).[7]

So far as their public role is concerned, proponents of sociology as a population science should then be well placed to take on the responsibility that Weber demanded. Since they start out from a recognition of individual variability and human population heterogeneity,

---

[7] Weber's criticism was directed equally at professors who were fervent German nationalists, such as Treitschke and his followers, and at Schmoller and other *Kathedersozialisten* – even though Weber was himself always a nationalist and, while never a socialist, had sympathy with some social-democratic positions and policies. He was also, it should be added, well aware, from his own experience, of the difficulties and inner conflicts that were likely to follow from the principled position he advocated when the same individual wished to be *both* a scientific *and* a political actor (see e.g. Mommsen, 1984: chs 7 and 8 esp.).

they should have little difficulty in accepting heterogeneity in, and conflict between, values – Weber's 'unceasing struggle' of 'warring gods' – as an aspect of the human condition from which they, no more than anyone else, can escape. And since their concern is to investigate the social regularities emergent in human populations and their underlying causal processes through methods that, they can maintain, are those most fit for this purpose, they are in a strong position to challenge, where necessary, those who seek to shore up their value positions and their associated sociopolitical objectives with sociology of a less well-founded kind.

References

Abbott, A. 1992. 'What do cases do? Some notes on activity in sociological analysis', in C. C. Ragin and H. S. Becker (eds), *What is a case?* Cambridge: Cambridge University Press.

Abbott, A. 1995. 'Sequence analysis: new methods for old ideas', *Annual Review of Sociology* 21: 93–113.

Abbott, A. 2001. *Chaos of disciplines*. Chicago, IL: University of Chicago Press.

Abbott, A. and Tsay, A. 2000. 'Sequence analysis and optimal matching methods in sociology', *Sociological Methods and Research* 29: 3–33.

Abrams, P. 1980. *Historical sociology*. Bath: Open Books.

Achen, C. H. 1982. *Interpreting and using regression*. Beverly Hills, CA: Sage.

Achen, C. H. 2005. 'Two cheers for Charles Ragin', *Studies in Comparative International Development*, 40: 27–32.

Aisenbrey, S. and Fasang, A. E. 2010. 'New life for old ideas: the "second wave" of sequence analysis bringing the "course" back into the life course', *Sociological Methods and Research* 38: 420–62.

Atkinson, A. 2008. *The changing distribution of earnings in OECD countries*. New York: Oxford University Press.

Atkinson, A. and Piketty, T. 2010. *Top incomes: a global perspective*. Oxford: Oxford University Press.

Augier, M. and March, J. G. (eds) 2004. *Models of man: essays in memory of Herbert A. Simon*. Cambridge, MA: MIT Press.

Baines, D. and Johnson, P. 1999. 'In search of the "traditional" working class: social mobility and occupational continuity in interwar London', *Economic History Review* 52: 692–713.

Baron-Cohen, S. 1991. 'Precursors to a theory of mind: understanding attention in others', in A. Whiten (ed.), *Natural theories of mind*. Oxford: Blackwell.

Baron-Cohen, S. 1995. *Mindblindness: an essay on autism and theory of mind*. Cambridge, MA: MIT Press.

Barrett, L., Dunbar, R. I. M. and Lycett, J. 2002. *Human evolutionary psychology*. Basingstoke: Palgrave.

Becker, R. 2003. 'Educational expansion and persistent inequalities of education in Germany', *European Sociological Review* 19: 1–24.

Bell, C. and Newby, H. (eds) 1974. *The sociology of community*. London: Frank Cass.

Bennett A. 2008. 'Process tracing: a Bayesian perspective', in J. M. Box-Steffensmeier, H. E. Brady and D. Collier (eds), *The Oxford Handbook of Political Methodology*. Oxford: Oxford University Press.

Berg, N. and Gigerenzer, G. 2010. 'As-if behavioural economics: neoclassical economics in disguise?', *History of Economic Ideas* 18: 133–65.

Berk, R. A. 2004. *Regression analysis: a constructive critique*. Thousand Oaks, CA: Sage.

Billari, F. C. 2005. 'Life course analysis: two (complementary) cultures?', *Advances in Life Course Research* 10: 261–81.

Billari, F. C. 2015. 'Integrating macro- and micro-level approaches in the explanation of population change', *Population Studies* 69: S11–20.

Bird, A. and Tobin, E. 2012. 'Natural kinds', *Stanford Encyclopedia of Philosophy*. http://plato.stanford.edu/archive/win2012/entries/natural-kinds/ (last accessed 1 May 2015).

Blalock, H. M. 1961. *Causal inferences in non-experimental research*. New York: Norton.

Blanden, J., Wilson, K., Haveman, R. and Smeeding, T. M. 2010. 'Understanding the mechanisms behind intergenerational persistence: a comparison of the United States and Great Britain', in T. M. Smeeding, R. Erikson and M. Jäntti (eds), *Persistence, privilege, and parenting*. New York: Russell Sage Foundation.

Blau, P. M. and Duncan, O. D. 1967. *The American occupational structure*. New York: Wiley.

Blaug, M. 1992. *The methodology of economics*, 2nd edn. Cambridge: Cambridge University Press.

Blossfeld, H.-P. and Prein, G. (eds) 1998. *Rational choice theory and large-scale data analysis*. Boulder, CO: Westview Press.

Blossfeld, H.-P. and Hofmeister, H. (eds) 2006. *Globalization, uncertainty and women's careers*. Cheltenham: Edward Elgar.

Blossfeld, H.-P., Mills, M. and Bernhardi, F. (eds) 2006. *Globalization, uncertainty and men's careers*. Cheltenham: Edward Elgar.

Blumer, H. 1956. 'Sociological analysis and the "variable"', *American Sociological Review* 21: 683–90.

Bohrnstedt, G. W. 2010. 'Measurement models for survey research', in P. V. Marsden and J. D. Wright (eds), *Handbook of survey research*, 2nd edn. Bingley: Emerald.

Booth, C. 1889–1903. *Life and labour of the people of London*. London: Macmillan.

Boudon, R. 1987. 'The individualistic tradition in sociology', in J. C. Alexander, B. Giesen, R. Münch and N. J. Smelser (eds), *The micro-macro link*. Berkeley, CA: University of California Press.

Boudon, R. 1990. 'Individualism and holism in the social sciences', in P. Birnbaum and J. Leca (eds), *Individualism*. Oxford: Oxford University Press.

Boudon, R. 1996. 'The "cognitivist model": a generalised "rational choice" model', *Rationality and Society* 8: 123–50.

Boudon, R. 2003a. *Raison, bonnes raisons*. Paris: PUF.

Boudon, R. 2003b. *Y-a-t-il encore une sociologie?* Paris: Odile Jacob.

Bowley, A. L. 1906. 'Address to the economic science and statistics section of the British Association for the Advancement of Science', *Journal of the Royal Statistical Society* 47: 607–25.

Bowley, A. L. and Burnett-Hurst, A. R. 1915. *Livelihood and poverty*. London: Bell.

Boyd, P. and Richerson, P. J. 1999. 'Norms and bounded rationality', in G. Gigerenzer and R. Selten (eds), *Bounded rationality: the adaptive toolbox*. Cambridge, MA: MIT Press.

Brady, H. E., Collier, D. and Seawright, J. 2006. 'Toward a pluralistic vision of methodology', *Political Analysis* 14: 353–68.

Breen, R. (ed.) 2004. *Social mobility in Europe*. Oxford: Oxford University Press.

Breen, R. and Goldthorpe, J. H. 1997. 'Explaining educational differentials: towards a formal rational action theory', *Rationality and Society* 9: 275–305.

Breen, R. and Yaish, M. 2006. 'Testing the Breen-Goldthorpe model of educational decision-making', in S. Morgan, D. B. Grusky and G. S. Fields (eds), *Mobility and inequality: frontiers of research from sociology and economics*. Stanford, CA: Stanford University Press.

Breen, R., van de Werfhorst, H. and Jaeger, M. M. 2014. 'Deciding under doubt: a theory of risk aversion, time discounting preferences and educational decision-making', *European Sociological Review* 30: 258–73.

Breiman, L. 2001. 'Statistical modelling: the two cultures' (with discussion), *Statistical Science* 16: 199–231.

Bruni, L. and Sugden, R. 2007. 'The road not taken: how psychology was removed from economics and how it might be brought back', *Economic Journal* 117: 146–73.

Buis, M. L. 2013. 'The composition of family background: the influence of the economic and cultural resources of both parents on the offspring's educational attainment in the Netherlands between 1939 and 1981', *European Sociological Review* 29: 593–602.

Bukodi, E. 2012. 'The relationship between work history and partnership formation in cohorts of British men born in 1958 and 1970', *Population Studies* 66: 123–45.

Bukodi, E. and Goldthorpe, J. H. 2013. 'Decomposing "social origins": the effects of parents' class, status and education on the educational attainment of their children', *European Sociological Review* 29: 1024–39.

Bukodi, E., Erikson, R. and Goldthorpe, J. H. 2014. 'The effects of social origins and cognitive ability on educational attainment: evidence from Britain and Sweden', *Acta Sociologica* 57: 293–310.

Bukodi, E., Goldthorpe, J. H., Waller, L. and Kuha, J. 2014. 'The mobility problem in Britain: new findings from the analysis of birth cohort data', *British Journal of Sociology* 66: 93–117.

Bukodi, E., Waller, L., Goldthorpe, J. H. and Halpin, B. 2015. 'Is education now class destiny? Class histories across three British birth cohorts'. Workshop on Algorithmic Methods in Social Research, Nuffield College, Oxford.

Burawoy, M. 2004. 'Manifesto for public sociology', *Social Problems* 51: 124–30.

Burawoy, M. 2005. 'For public sociology', *American Sociological Review* 70: 4–28.

Byrne, D. 2012. 'UK sociology and quantitative methods: are we as weak as they think? Or are they barking up the wrong tree?', *Sociology* 46: 13–24.

Carmines, E. G. and Zeller, R. A. 1979. *Reliability and validity assessment*. Beverly Hills, CA: Sage.

Carrithers, M. 1992. *Why humans have cultures*. Oxford: Oxford University Press.

Cartwright, N. 2007. *Hunting causes and using them*. Cambridge: Cambridge University Press.

Cartwright, N. and Hardie, J. 2012. *Evidence-based policy*. Oxford: Oxford University Press.

Castellani, B. 2014. 'Complexity and the failure of quantitative social science', *Discover Society*. http://www.discoversociety.org/2014/11/04/focus-complexity-and-the-failure-of-quantitative-social-science/ (last accessed 1 May 2015).

Chan, T.-W. (ed.) 2010. *Social status and cultural consumption*. Cambridge: Cambridge University Press.

Chan, T.-W. and Goldthorpe, J. H. 2007. 'Class and status: the conceptual distinction and its empirical relevance', *American Sociological Review* 72: 512–32.

Christakis, N. and Fowler, J. 2010. *Connected*. London: Harper.

Clark, C. 2013. *The sleepwalkers: how Europe went to war in 1914*. London: Penguin.

Clawson, D., Zussman, R., Misra, J., Gerstel, N., Stokes, R. and Anderton, D. L. (eds) 2007. *Public sociology*. Berkeley, CA: University of California Press.

Cobban, A. 1965. *The social interpretation of the French revolution*. Cambridge: Cambridge University Press.

Cochran, W. G. 1965. 'The planning of observational studies of human populations', *Journal of the Royal Statistical Society*, Series A 128: 234–66.

Cole, S. 1994. 'Why sociology doesn't make progress like the natural sciences', *Sociological Forum* 9: 133–54.

Coleman, J. S. 1986. 'Social theory, social research, and a theory of action', *American Journal of Sociology* 91: 1309–35.

Coleman, J. S. 1990. *Foundations of social theory*. Cambridge, MA: Belknap.

Collier, D., Brady, H. E. and Seawright, J. 2004. 'Sources of leverage in causal inference: towards and alternative view of methodology', in H. E. Brady and D. Collier (eds), *Rethinking social inquiry*. Lanham: Rowmanand Littlefield.

Cooper, B. 2005. 'Applying Ragin's crisp and fuzzy set QCA to large datasets: social class and educational achievement in the National Child Development Study', *Sociological Research Online*. http://www.socresonline.org.uk/10/2/cooper1.html (last accessed 1 May 2015).

Cornfield, J., Haenszel, W., Hammond, E. C., Lilienfeld, A. M., Shimkin, M. B. and Wynder, E. L. 1959. 'Smoking and lung cancer: recent evidence and a discussion of some questions', *Journal of the National Cancer Institute* 22: 173–203.

Couper, M. P. 2013. 'Is the sky falling? New technology, changing media, and the future of surveys', *Survey Research Methods* 7: 145–56.

Cox, D. R. 1992. 'Causality: some statistical aspects', *Journal of the Royal Statistical Society* Series A 155: 291–301.

Cox, D. R. 2001. 'Comment' on Breiman (2001).

Cox, D. R. and Wermuth, N. 1996. *Multivariate dependencies: models, analysis and interpretation*. London: Chapman and Hall.

Cox, D. R. and Donnelly, C. A. 2011. *Principles of applied statistics*. Cambridge: Cambridge University Press.

Dahrendorf, R. 1959. *Class and class conflict in industrial society*. London: Routledge.

Dalal, S. R., Fowlkes, E. B. and Hoadley, B. 1989. 'Risk analysis of the space shuttle: pre-Challenger prediction of failure', *Journal of the American Statistical Association* 84: 945–57.

Davidson, D. 1980. *Essays on actions and events*. Oxford: Clarendon Press.

Davies, R., Heinesen, E. and Holm, A. 2002. 'The relative risk aversion hypothesis of educational choice', *Journal of Population Economics* 15: 683–713.

Davis, K. and Moore, W. E. 1945. 'Some principles of stratification', *American Sociological Review* 10: 242–9.

Deaton, A. 2010. 'Instruments, randomization, and learning about development', *Journal of Economic Literature* 48: 424–55.

Dennett, D. C. 1995. *Darwin's dangerous idea*. London: Allen Lane.

Desrosières, A. 1991. 'The part in relation to the whole: how to generalise? The pre-history of representative sampling', in M. Bulmer, K. Bales and K. K. Sklar (eds), *The social survey in historical perspective, 1880–1940*. Cambridge: Cambridge University Press.

Desrosières, A. 1993. *La politique des grands nombres*. Paris: La Découverte.

DiPrete, T. A. and Eirich, G. M. 2006. 'Cumulative advantage as a mechanism for inequality: a review of theory and evidence', *Annual Review of Sociology* 32: 271–97.

Dunbar, R. I. M. 2000. 'Causal reasoning, mental rehearsal and the evolution of primate cognition', in C. Heyes and L. Huber (eds), *The evolution of cognition*. Cambridge, MA: MIT Press.

Dunbar, R. I. M. 2004. *The human story: a new history of mankind's evolution*. London: Faber and Faber.

Dunbar, R. I. M. 2014. *Human evolution*. London: Pelican Books.

Duncan, O. D. 1961. 'A socioeconomic index for all occupations', in A. J. Reiss (ed.), *Occupations and social status*. New York: Free Press.

Duncan, O. D. 1975. *Introduction to structural equation models*. New York: Academic Press.

Duncan, O. D. 1984. *Notes on social measurement*. New York: Russell Sage.

Duncan, O. D. 1992. 'What if?', *Contemporary Sociology* 21: 667–8.

Durkheim, E. 1895/1938. *The rules of sociological method*. Glencoe, IL: Free Press.

Durkheim, E. 1897/1952. *Suicide*. London: Routledge and Kegan Paul.

Edgerton, R. B. 1992. *Sick societies: challenging the myth of primitive harmony*. New York: Free Press.

Edgeworth, F. Y. 1885. 'Observations and statistics: an essay on the theory of errors and the first principles of statistics', *Transactions of the Cambridge Philosophical Society* 14: 138–69.

Elster, J. 1979. *Ulysses and the sirens*. Cambridge: Cambridge University Press.

Elster, J. 1983. *Sour grapes*. Cambridge: Cambridge University Press.

Elster, J. 1989. *Nuts and bolts for the social sciences*. Cambridge: Cambridge University Press.

Elster, J. 1997. 'More than enough', *University of Chicago Law Review* 64: 748–64.

Elster, J. 1998. 'A plea for mechanisms', in P. Hedström and R. Swedberg (eds), *Social mechanisms*. Cambridge: Cambridge University Press.

Elster, J. 2007. *Explaining social behavior*. Cambridge: Cambridge University Press.

Epstein, J. M. 2006. *Generative social science*. Princeton, NJ: Princeton University Press.

Erikson, R. 1998. 'Thresholds and mechanisms', in H.-P. Blossfeld and G. Prein (eds), *Rational choice theory and large-scale data analysis*. Boulder, CO: Westview.

Erikson, R. and Goldthorpe, J. H. 1992. *The constant flux*. Oxford: Clarendon Press.

Erikson, R. and Jonsson, J. O. 1996. 'Explaining class inequality in education: the Swedish test case', in R. Erikson and J. O. Jonsson (eds), *Can education be equalized?* Boulder, CO: Westview.

Erikson, R., Goldthorpe, J. H. and Hällsten, M. 2012. 'No way back up from ratcheting down? A critique of the "microclass" approach to the analysis of social mobility', *Acta Sociologica* 55: 211–29.

Esser, H. 1996. 'What is wrong with variable sociology?', *European Sociological Review* 12: 159–66.

Esser, H. 1999. *Soziologie. Spezielle Grundlagen. Band 1: Situationslogik und Handeln*. Frankfurt: Campus.

Evans, G. and De Graaf, N. D. (eds) 2013. *Political choice matters*. Oxford: Oxford University Press.

Ferri, E., Bynner, J. and Wadsworth, M. 2003. *Changing Britain, changing lives: three generations at the turn of the century*. London: Institute of Education.

Fisher, R. A. 1922. 'On the dominance ratio', *Proceedings of the Royal Society of Edinburgh* 52: 321–41.

Fisher, R. A. 1925. *Statistical methods for research workers*. Edinburgh: Oliver and Boyd.

Frankenberg, R. 1966. *Communities in Britain*. Harmondsworth: Penguin.

Freedman, D. A. 1991. 'Statistical analysis and shoe leather', *Sociological Methodology* 21: 291–313.

Freedman, D. A. 1992. 'As others see us: a case study in path analysis', in J. P. Shaffer (ed.), *The role of models in nonexperimental social science: two debates*. Washington, DC: American Educational Research Association and American Statistical Association.

Freedman, D. A. 1997. 'From association to causation via regression', in V. R. McKim and S. P. Turner (eds), *Causality in crisis?* Notre Dame: Notre Dame University Press.

Freedman, D. A. 2010. *Statistical models and causal inference: a dialogue with the social sciences*. Cambridge: Cambridge University Press.

Galea, S. and Link, B. G. 2013. 'Six paths for the future of social epidemiology', *American Journal of Epidemiology* 178: 843–49.

Galton, F. 1889a. *Natural inheritance*. London: Macmillan.

Galton, F. 1889b. 'Comments' on Tylor (1889).

Gambetta, D. 2009. 'Signalling', in P. Hedström and P. Bearman (eds), *The Oxford handbook of analytical sociology*. Oxford: Oxford University Press.

Gärdenfors, P. 2006. *How Homo became sapiens*. Oxford: Oxford University Press.

Gelman, A. 2011. 'Causality and statistical learning', *American Journal of Sociology* 117: 955–66.

Gelman, A. and Imbens, G. 2013. 'Why ask why? Forward causal inference and reverse causal questions'. National Bureau of Economic Research Working Paper 19614.

George, A. L. and Bennett, A. 2005. *Case studies and theory development in the social sciences*. Cambridge, MA: MIT Press.

Giddens, A. 1979. *Central problems in social theory*. London: Macmillan.

Giddens, A. 1984. *The constitution of society*. Cambridge: Polity Press.

Gigerenzer, G. 2008. *Rationality for mortals*. Oxford: Oxford University Press.

Gigerenzer, G. and Selten, R. (eds) 1999. *Bounded rationality: the adaptive toolbox*. Cambridge, MA: MIT Press.

Gigerenzer, G. and Todd, P. M. 1999. 'Fast and frugal heuristics: the adaptive toolbox', in G. Gigerenzer and P. M. Todd (eds), *Simple heuristics that make us smart*. New York: Oxford University Press.

Gigerenzer, G., Swijtink, Z., Porter, T., Daston, L., Beatty, J. and Krüger, L. 1989. *The empire of chance*. Cambridge: Cambridge University Press.

Gillispie, C. C. 1963. 'Intellectual factors in the background of analysis by probabilities', in A. C. Crombie (ed.), *Scientific change*. New York: Basic Books.

Ginsberg, M. 1965. 'Introduction' to 1965 reprint of Hobhouse, Wheeler and Ginsberg (1915).

Glass, D. V. 1973. *Numbering the people*. Farnborough: Saxon House.

Goertz, G. and Mahoney, J. 2009. 'Scope in case study research', in D. Byrne and C. C. Ragin (eds), *The Sage handbook of case-based methods*. Los Angeles: Sage.

Goldstone, J. A. 1995. 'Predicting revolutions: why we could (and should) have foreseen the revolutions of 1989–91 in the USSR and Eastern Europe', in N. R. Keddie (ed.), *Debating revolutions*. New York: New York University Press.

Goldstone J. A. 2003. 'Comparative historical analysis and knowledge accumulation in the study of revolutions', in J. Mahoney and D. Rueschemeyer (eds), *Comparative historical analysis in the social sciences*. Cambridge: Cambridge University Press.

Goldthorpe, J. H. 1987. *Social mobility and class structure in modern Britain*, 2nd edn. Oxford: Clarendon Press.

Goldthorpe, J. H. 1994. 'The uses of history in sociology: a reply', *British Journal of Sociology* 45: 55–77.

Goldthorpe, J. H. 1996. 'Class analysis and the reorientation of class theory: the case of persisting differentials in educational attainment', *British Journal of Sociology* 47: 481–505.

Goldthorpe, J. H. 2007. *On sociology*, 2nd edn, 2 vols. Stanford, CA: Stanford University Press.

Goldthorpe, J. H. 2012. 'Back to class and status: or why a sociological view of social inequality should be re-asserted', *Revista española de investigaciones sociológicas* 137: 1–16.

Goldthorpe, J. H. 2013. 'Understanding – and misunderstanding – social mobility: the entry of the economists, the confusion of politicians and the limits of educational policy', *Journal of Social Policy* 42: 431–50.

Goldthorpe, J. H. 2014. 'The role of education in intergenerational social mobility: problems from empirical research in sociology and some theoretical pointers from economics', *Rationality and Society* 26: 265–89.

Goldthorpe, J. H., Lockwood, D., Bechhofer, F. and Platt, J. 1969. *The affluent worker in the class structure*. Cambridge: Cambridge University Press.

Goodman, L. A. 2007a. 'Statistical magic and/or statistical serendipity: an age of progress in the analysis of categorical data', *Annual Review of Sociology* 33: 1–19.

Goodman, L. A. 2007b. 'Otis Dudley Duncan, quantitative sociologist par excellence: path analysis, loglinear methods, and Rasch models', *Research in Social Stratification and Mobility* 25: 129–39.

Granovetter, M. 1995. *Getting a job: a study of contacts and careers*, 2nd edn. Chicago, IL: University of Chicago Press.

Grusky, D. B. and Hauser, R. M. 1984. 'Comparative social mobility revisited: models of divergence and convergence in 16 countries', *American Sociological Review* 49: 19–38.

Haack, S. 1998. *Manifesto of a passionate moderate*. Chicago, IL: University of Chicago Press.

Hacking, I. 1987. 'Was there a probabilistic revolution, 1800–1930?', in L. Krüger, L. J. Daston and M. Heidelberger (eds), *The probabilistic revolution*, vol. 1. Cambridge, MA: MIT Press.

Hacking, I. 1990. *The taming of chance*. Cambridge: Cambridge University Press.

Hacking, I. 2000. *The social construction of what?* Cambridge, MA: Harvard University Press.

Halbwachs, M. 1912. *La classe ouvrière et les niveaux de vie*. Paris: Alcan.

Halpin, B. and Chan, T.-W. 1998. 'Class careers as sequences: an optimal matching of work-life histories', *European Sociological Review* 14, 111–29.

Hart, N. 1989. 'Gender and the rise and fall of class politics', *New Left Review* I/175: 19–47.

Hart, N. 1994. 'John Goldthorpe and the relics of sociology', *British Journal of Sociology* 45: 21–30.

Hauser, R. M. and Warren, J. R. 1997. 'Socioeconomic indexes for occupations: a review, update and critique', *Sociological Methodology* 44: 203–18.

Hausman, D. M. 1992. *The inexact and separate science of economics*. Cambridge: Cambridge University Press.

Hechter, M. 1995. 'Reflections on historical prophecy in the social sciences', *American Journal of Sociology* 100: 1520–7.

Hedström, P. 2005. *Dissecting the social*. Cambridge: Cambridge University Press.

Hedström, P. and Swedberg, R. 1998a. 'Social mechanisms: an introductory essay', in P. Hedström and R. Swedberg (eds), *Social mechanisms*. Cambridge: Cambridge University Press.

Hedström, P. and Swedberg, R. (eds) 1998b. *Social mechanisms*. Cambridge: Cambridge University Press.

Hedström, P. and Bearman, P. 2009a. 'What is analytical sociology all about? An introductory essay', in P. Hedström and P. Bearman (eds), *The Oxford handbook of analytical sociology*. Oxford: Oxford University Press.

Hedström, P. and Bearman, P. (eds) 2009b. *The Oxford handbook of analytical sociology*. Oxford: Oxford University Press.

Hempel, C. G. 1965. *Aspects of scientific explanation*. New York: Free Press.

Hobhouse, L. T., Wheeler, G. C. and Ginsberg, M. 1915. *The material culture and social institutions of the simpler peoples*. London: Chapman and Hall.

Hogben, L. (ed.) 1938. *Political arithmetic*. London: Allen and Unwin.

Holland, P. 1986. 'Statistics and causal inference', *Journal of the American Statistical Association* 81: 945–60.

Hollis, M. 1977. *Models of man*. Cambridge: Cambridge University Press.

Hollis, M. 1987. *The cunning of reason*. Cambridge: Cambridge University Press.

Holm, A. and Jaeger, M. M. 2008. 'Does relative risk aversion explain educational inequality? A dynamic choice approach', *Research in Social Stratification and Mobility* 26: 199–219.

Homans, G. C. 1964. 'Bringing men back in', *American Sociological Review* 29: 809–18.

Hope, K. 1984. *As others see us: schooling and social mobility in Scotland and the United States*. Cambridge: Cambridge University Press.

Hoselitz, B. F. 1952. *The progress of underdeveloped areas*. Chicago, IL: Chicago University Press.

Hox, J. J. 2010. *Multilevel analysis*. New York: Routledge.

Hug, S. 2013. 'Qualitative comparative analysis: How inductive use and measurement error lead to problematic inference', *Political Analysis* 21: 252–65.

Illari, P. M., Russo, F. and Williamson, J. (eds) 2011. *Causality in the sciences.* Oxford: Oxford University Press.

Inglehart, R. and Norris, P. 2003. *Rising tide: gender equality and cultural change around the world.* Cambridge: Cambridge University Press.

Ishida, H. (ed.) 2008. *Social stratification and social mobility in late-industrializing countries.* Tokyo: SSM Research Series 14.

Jablonka, E. and Lamb, M. J. 2005. *Evolution in four dimensions.* Cambridge, MA: MIT Press.

Jackson, M. V. (ed.) 2013. *Determined to succeed: performance versus choice in educational attainment.* Stanford, CA: Stanford University Press.

Jaeger, M. M. 2007. 'Educational mobility across three generations: the changing impact of parental social class, economic, social and cultural capital', *European Sociological Review* 9: 527–50.

Jencks, C. 1972. *Inequality.* New York: Basic Books.

Jencks, C. 1979. *Who gets ahead?* New York: Basic Books.

Jonsson, J. O., Grusky, D. B., Di Carlo, M., Pollak, R. and Brinton, M. C. 2009. 'Microclass mobility: social reproduction in four countries', *American Journal of Sociology* 114: 977–1036.

Kaberry, P. 1957. 'Malinowski's contribution to field-work methods and the writing of ethnography', in R. Firth (ed.), *Man and culture: an evaluation of the work of Bronislaw Malinowski.* London: Routledge and Kegan Paul.

Kahneman, D. 2011. *Thinking fast and slow.* London: Penguin.

Kahneman, D. and Tversky, A. 1979. 'Prospect theory: an analysis of decision under risk', *Econometrica* 47: 263–91.

Kendall, P. L. and Lazarsfeld, P. F. 1950. 'Problems of survey analysis', in R. K. Merton and P. F. Lazarsfeld (eds), *Continuities in social research: studies in the scope and method of 'The American Soldier'.* Glencoe, IL: Free Press.

Kerr, C., Dunlop, J. T., Harbison, F. H. and Myers, C. A. 1960. *Industrialism and industrial man.* Cambridge, MA: Harvard University Press.

Kiaer, A. N. 1895–96. 'Observations et expériences concernant des dénombrements représentatifs', *Bulletin of the International Statistical Institute* 9: 176–83.

Kiaer, A. N. 1903. 'Sur les méthodes représentatives ou typologique', *Bulletin of the International Statistical Institute* 13: 66–70.

Kincaid, H. 2011. 'Causal modelling, mechanism, and probability in epidemiology', in P. M. Illari, F. Russo and J. Williamson (eds), *Causality in the sciences.* Oxford: Oxford University Press.

King, G., Keohane, R. O. and Verba, S. 1994. *Designing social inquiry*. Princeton, NJ: Princeton University Press.

Kroeber, A. L. 1917. 'The superorganic', *American Anthropologist* 19: 208–13.

Krogslund, C., Choi, D. D. and Poertner, M. 2015. 'Fuzzy sets on shaky grounds: parameter sensitivity and confirmation bias in fsQCA', *Political Analysis* 23: 21–41.

Krüger, L. 1987. 'The slow rise of probabilism: philosophical arguments in the nineteenth century', in Krüger, L., Daston, L. J. and Heidelberger, M. (eds), *The probabilistic revolution*, vol. 1. Cambridge, MA: MIT Press.

Krüger, L., Daston, L. J. and Heidelberger, M. (eds) 1987. *The probabilistic revolution*, vol. 1. Cambridge, MA: MIT Press.

Krüger, L., Gigerenzer, G. and Morgan, M. S. (eds) 1987. *The probabilistic revolution*, vol. 2. Cambridge, MA: MIT Press.

Kruskal, W. and Mosteller, F. 1980. 'Representative sampling, IV: the history of the concept in statistics, 1895–1939', *International Statistical Review* 48: 169–95.

Kumar, M. 2008. *Quantum*. Cambridge: Icon Books.

Kuper, A. 1973. *Anthropologists and anthropology*. London: Allen Lane.

Laland, K. N. 1999. 'Imitation, social learning and preparedness as mechanisms of bounded rationality', in G. Gigerenzer, and R. Selten (eds), *Bounded rationality: the adaptive toolbox*. Cambridge, MA: MIT Press.

Laplace, P. S. 1814/1951. *A philosophical essay on probabilities*. New York: Dover.

Laslett, P. 1972. 'Introduction: the history of the family', in P. Laslett (ed.), *Household and family in past time*. Cambridge: Cambridge University Press.

Latour, B. 2000. 'On the partial existence of existing and nonexisting objects', in L. Daston (ed.), *Biographies of scientific objects*. Chicago, IL: University of Chicago Press.

Lazarsfeld, P. F. 1955. 'Interpretation of statistical relations as a research operation', in P. F. Lazarsfeld and M. Rosenberg (eds), *The Language of social research*, Glencoe, IL: Free Press.

Lazarsfeld, P. F. 1961. 'Notes on the history of quantification in sociology', *Isis* 52: 277–333.

Lazarsfeld, P. F. and Henry, N. W. 1968. *Latent structure analysis*. Boston, MA: Houghton Mifflin.

Lazer, D., Pentland, A., Adamic, L., Aral, S., Barabási, A.-L., Brewer, D. et al. 2009. 'Computational social science', *Science*, 323: 721–3.

Lazer, D., Kennedy, R., King, G. and Vespignani, A. 2014. 'The parable of Google flu: traps in big data analysis', *Science* 343: 1203–5.

Leach, E. R. 1957. 'The epistemological background to Malinowski's empiricism', in R. Firth (ed.), *Man and culture: an evaluation of the work of Bronislaw Malinowski*. London: Routledge and Kegan Paul.

Lee, R. D. 2001. 'Demography abandons its core'. Population Association of America, presentation at the Annual Meeting.

Leigh, A., Jencks, C. and Smeeding, T. M. 2009. 'Health and economic inequality', in W. Salverda and B. Nolan (eds), *The Oxford handbook of economic inequality*. Oxford: Oxford University Press.

Le Play, F. 1877–79. *Les ouvriers européens*, 2nd edn. Tours: Alfred Mame.

Lerner, D. 1964. *The passing of traditional society*. London: Collier-Macmillan.

Lesthaeghe, R. 2010. 'The unfolding story of the second demographic transition', *Population and Development Review* 36: 211–51.

Levine, J. H. 2000. 'But what have you done for us lately? Commentary on Abbott and Tsay', *Sociological Methods and Research* 29: 34–40.

Lie, E. 2002. 'The rise and fall of sample surveys in Norway', *Science in Context* 15: 385–409.

Lieberson, S. 1987. *Making it count*. Berkeley, CA: University of California Press.

Lieberson, S. 2004. 'Comments on the use and utility of QCA', *Qualitative Methods* 2: 13–14.

Lieberson, S. and Lynn, F. B. 2002. 'Barking up the wrong branch: scientific alternatives to the current model of sociological science', *Annual Review of Sociology* 28: 1–19.

Lipset, S. M., Trow, M. and Coleman, J. S. 1956. *Union democracy*. New York: Free Press.

Lockwood, D. 1956. 'Some remarks on "The Social System"', *British Journal of Sociology* 7: 134–46.

Lockwood, D. 1992. *Solidarity and schism*. Oxford: Oxford University Press.

Louçã, F. 2008. 'The widest cleft in statistics: how and why Fisher opposed Neyman and Pearson'. Lisbon: Istituto Superior de Economia e Gestão, Working Paper 2–2008/DE/UECE.

Lucas, S. R. and Szatrowski, A. 2014. 'Qualitative comparative analysis in critical perspective', *Sociological Methodology* 44: 1–79.

Lynch, J., Smith, G. D., Harper, S., Hillemeier, M., Ross, N., Kaplan, G. A. and Wolfson, M. 2004. 'Is income inequality a determinant of population health?', *Millbank Quarterly* 82: 5–99 and 355–400.

Lyons, R. 2011. 'The spread of evidence-poor medicine via flawed social-network analysis', *Statistics, Policy and Politics* 2: 1–26.

Mackie, J. L. 1974. *The cement of the universe: a study of causation*. Oxford: Clarendon Press.

Mahon, B. 2003. *The man who changed everything: the life of James Clerk Maxwell*. Chichester: Wiley.

Mahoney, J. and Goertz, G. 2006. 'A tale of two cultures: contrasting quantitative and qualitative research', *Political Analysis* 14: 227–49.

Mahoney, J. and Larkin Terrie, P. 2008. 'Comparative-historical analysis in contemporary political science', in J. M. Box-Steffensmeier, H. E. Brady and D. Collier (eds), *The Oxford handbook of political methodology*. Oxford: Oxford University Press.

Mahoney, J., Kimball, E. and Koivu, K. L. 2009. 'The logic of historical explanation in the social sciences', *Comparative Political Studies* 42: 114–46.

Malinowski, B. 1926. *Crime and custom in savage society*. New York: Kegan Paul, Trench and Trubner.

Manning, R., Levine, M. and Collins, A. 2007. 'The Kitty Genovese murder and the social psychology of helping: the parable of the 38 witnesses', *American Psychologist* 6: 555–62.

Manting, D. 1996. 'The changing meaning of cohabitation and marriage', *European Sociological Review* 12: 53–65.

Marsh, C. 1982. *The survey method: the contribution of surveys to sociological explanation*. London: Allen and Unwin.

Marshall, G., Newby, H., Rose, D. and Vogler, C. 1988. *Social class in modern Britain*. London: Hutchinson.

Marx, A. 2010. 'Crisp-set qualitative comparative analysis (csQCA) and model specification: benchmarks for future csQCA applications', *International Journal of Multiple Research Approaches* 4: 138–58.

Mayer-Schönberger, V. and Cukier, K. 2013. *Big data*. London: John Murray.

Mayr, E. 1982. *The growth of biological thought*. Cambridge, MA: Harvard University Press.

Mayr, E. 2001. 'The philosophical foundations of Darwinism', *Proceedings of the American Philosophical Society* 145: 488–95.

McCutcheon, A. L. and Mills, C. 1998. 'Categorical data analysis: log-linear and latent class models', in E. Scarborough and E. Tanenbaum (eds), *Research strategies in the social sciences*. Oxford: Oxford University Press.

Mead, M. 1953. *Cultural patterns and technological change*. Paris: UNESCO.

Merton, R. K. 1957. *Social theory and social structure*, 2nd edn. Glencoe, IL: Free Press.

Merton, R. K. 1959. 'Notes on problem finding in sociology', in R. K. Merton, L. Broom and L. S. Cottrell (eds), *Sociology today: problems and prospects*. New York: Harper and Row.

Merton, R. K. 1987. 'Three fragments from a sociologist's notebook: establishing the phenomenon, specified ignorance and strategic research materials', *Annual Review of Sociology* 13: 1–28.

Mill, J. S. 1843/1973–74. *A system of logic ratiocinative and inductive*, in J. M. Robson (ed.), *Collected works of John Stuart Mill*. Toronto, ON: Toronto University Press.

Mills, C. 2014. 'The great British class fiasco', *Sociology* 48: 437–44.

Mills, M., Blossfeld, H.-P. and Klijzing, E. 2005. 'Becoming an adult in uncertain times', in H.-P. Blossfeld, E. Klijzing, M. Mills and K. Kurz (eds), *Globalization, uncertainty and youth in society*. London: Routledge.

Mitchell, J. C. 1969. *Social networks in urban situations: analysis of personal relations in central African towns*. Manchester: Manchester University Press.

Mommsen, W. J. 1984. *Max Weber and German politics 1890–1920*. Chicago, IL: University of Chicago Press.

Monod, J. 1970. *Le hazard et la nécessité*. Paris: Le Seuil.

Morgan, M. S. 2014. 'Case studies', in N. Cartwright and E. Montuschi (eds), *Philosophy of Social Science*. Oxford: Oxford University Press.

Morgan, S. L. and Winship, C. 2007. *Counterfactuals and causal Inference*. Cambridge: Cambridge University Press.

Morrison, M. 2002. 'Modelling populations: Pearson and Fisher on Mendelism and biometry', *British Journal of Philosophy of Science* 53: 39–68.

Murdock, G. P. 1949. *Social structure*. New York: Macmillan.

Murdock, G. P. 1965. *Culture and society*. Pittsburgh, PA: University of Pittsburgh Press.

Nazio, T. 2008. *Cohabitation, family and society*. London: Routledge.

Nazio, T. and Blossfeld, H.-P. 2003. 'The diffusion of cohabitation among young women in West Germany, East Germany and Italy', *European Journal of Population* 19: 47–82.

Need, A. and de Jong, U. 2000. 'Educational differentials in the Netherlands: testing rational action theory', *Rationality and Society* 13: 71–98.

Neyman, J. 1934. 'On the two different aspects of the representative method: the method of stratified sampling and the method of purposive selection', *Journal of the Royal Statistical Society* 97: 558–606.

Neyman, J. 1952. *Lectures and conferences on mathematical statistics and probability*. Washington, DC: US Department of Agriculture.

Neyman, J. 1975. 'Study of chance mechanisms – a quasi-Copernican revolution in science and mathematics', in J. Neyman (ed.), *The heritage of Copernicus*. Cambridge, MA: MIT Press.

Ní Bhrolcháin, M. 2001. '"Divorce effects" and causality in the social sciences', *European Sociological Review* 17: 33–57.

Ní Bhrolcháin, M. and Dyson, T. 2007. 'On causation in demography: issues and illustrations', *Population and Development Review* 33: 1–36.

Nielsen, F. 2004. 'The vacant "we": remarks on public sociology', *Social Forces* 82: 1619–27.

Oppenheimer, V. K. 1994. 'Women's rising employment and the future of the family in industrial society', *Population and Development Review* 20: 293–342.

Oppenheimer, V. K. 1997. 'Men's career development and marriage timing during a period of rising inequality', *Demography* 34: 311–30.

Ostrom, E. 1990. *Governing the commons*. Cambridge: Cambridge University Press.

Ostrom, E. 2000. 'Collective action and the evolution of social norms', *Journal of Economic Perspectives* 14: 137–58.

Palloni, A. 1998. 'Theories and models of diffusion in sociology'. Centre for Demography and Ecology, University of Wisconsin-Madison, Working Paper 98–11.

Parsons, T. 1937. *The structure of social action*. Glencoe, IL: Free Press.

Parsons, T. 1940. 'An analytical approach to the theory of social stratification', *American Journal of Sociology* 45: 849–62.

Parsons, T. 1952. *The social system*. Glencoe, IL: Free Press.

Parsons, T. 1966. *Societies: evolutionary and comparative perspectives*. Englewood Cliffs, NJ: Prentice Hall.

Parsons, T. 1971. *The system of modern societies*. Englewood Cliffs, NJ: Prentice Hall.

Pavlinov, I. Y. 2013. *The species problem – ongoing issues*. Rijeka: InTech.

Pawson, R. and Tilley, N. 1997. *Realistic evaluation*. London: Sage.

Pearce, N. 1999. 'Epidemiology as a population science', *International Journal of Epidemiology* 28: S1015–18.

Pearce, N. 2011. 'Epidemiology in a changing world: variation, causation and ubiquitous risk factors', *International Journal of Epidemiology* 40: 503–12.

Pearl, J. 2000. *Causality: models, reasoning, and inference*. Cambridge: Cambridge University Press.

Pieckalkiewicz, J. 1934. *Rapport sur les recherches concernant la structure de la population ouvrière en Pologne selon la méthode representative*. Warsaw: Institute for Social Problems.

Piketty, T. 2014. *Capital in the twenty-first century*. Cambridge, MA: Harvard University Press.

Pinker, S. 2002. *The blank slate*. London: Allen Lane.

Platt, J. 1971. *Social research in Bethnal Green*. London: Macmillan.

Plotkin, H. 2007. 'The power of culture', in R. I. M. Dunbar and L. Barrett (eds), *The Oxford handbook of evolutionary psychology*. Oxford: Oxford University Press.

Popper, K. R. 1945. *The open society and its enemies*. London: Routledge and Kegan Paul.

Popper, K. R. 1957. *The poverty of historicism*. London: Routledge and Kegan Paul.

Popper, K. R. 1959. *The logic of scientific discovery*. London: Hutchinson.

Popper, K. R. 1972. *Objective knowledge*. Oxford: Clarendon Press.

Popper, K. R. 1994. *The myth of the framework*. London: Routledge.

Porter, T. 1982. 'A statistical survey of gases: Maxwell's social physics', *Historical Studies in the Physical Sciences* 8: 77–116.

Porter, T. 1986. *The rise of statistical thinking, 1820–1900*. Princeton, NJ: Princeton University Press.

Quetelet, A. 1835/1842. *A treatise on man and the development of his faculties*. Edinburgh: Chambers.

Quetelet, A. 1846. *Lettres à S. A. R. le Duc Régnant de Saxe-Coburg-Gotha, sur la théorie des probabilities, appliquée aux sciences morales et politiques*. Brussels: Hayez.

Quetelet, A. 1869. *Physique sociale*. Brussels: Murquardt.

Rabin, M. 1998. 'Psychology and economics', *Journal of Economic Literature*, 36: 11–46.

Ragin, C. C. 1987. *The comparative method*. Berkeley, CA: University of California Press.

Ragin, C. C. 2000. *Fuzzy-set social science*. Chicago, IL: University of Chicago Press.

Ragin, C. C. 2013. 'New directions in the logic of social inquiry', *Political Research Quarterly* 66: 171–4.

Ragin, C. C. and Rihoux, B. 2004. 'Replies to commentaries: reassurances and rebuttals', *Qualitative Methods* 2: 22–4.

Richards, A. I. 1957. 'The concept of culture in Malinowski's work', in R. Firth (ed.), *Man and culture: an evaluation of the work of Bronislaw Malinowski*. London: Routledge and Kegan Paul.

Richerson, P. J. and Boyd, R. 2005. *Not by genes alone*. Chicago, IL: University of Chicago Press.

Rihoux, B. and Marx, A. 2013. 'Qualitative comparative analysis at 25: state of play and agenda', *Political Research Quarterly* 66: 167–71.

Rose, D. and Harrison, E. 2010. *Social class in Europe: an introduction to the European Socio-Economic Classification*. London: Routledge.

Rose, D. and Pevalin, D. J. (eds) 2003. *A researcher's guide to the National Statistics Socio-Economic Classification*. London: Sage.

Rose, D. and Pevalin, D. J. (with O'Reilly, K.) 2005. *The National Statistics Socio-Economic Classification: origins, development and use*. London: Palgrave Macmillan.

Rosenbaum, P. R. 1995. *Observational studies*. New York: Springer.

Runciman, W. G. 1998. *The social animal*. London: Harper Collins.

Salganik, M. J. and Heckathorn, D. D. 2004. 'Sampling and estimation in hidden populations using respondent-driven sampling', *Sociological Methodology* 34: 193–239.

Savage, M. and Burrows, R. 2007. 'The coming crisis of empirical sociology', *Sociology* 41: 885–899.

Savage, M., Devine, F., Cunningham, N., Taylor, M., Li, Y., Hjellbrekke, J. et al. 2013. 'A new model of social class? Findings from the BBC's great class survey experiment', *Sociology* 47: 219–50.

Seawright, J. 2005. 'Qualitative comparative analysis vis-à-vis regression', *Studies in Comparative International Development* 40: 3–26.

Sen, A. K. 1986. 'Prediction and economic theory', *Proceedings of the Royal Society of London* A407: 3–23.

Silver, C. (ed.) 1982. *Frédéric Le Play on family, work and social change*. Chicago, IL: Chicago University Press.

Silver, N. 2012. *The signal and the noise*. London: Penguin.

Simon, H. A. 1982. *Models of bounded rationality*. Cambridge, MA: MIT Press.

Simon, H. A. 1983. *Reason in human affairs*. Oxford: Blackwell.

Skocpol, T. 1979. *States and social revolutions*. Cambridge: Cambridge University Press.

Smith, T. M. F. 1997. 'Social surveys and social science', *Canadian Journal of Statistics* 25: 23–44.

Sørensen, A. B. 1998. 'Theoretical mechanisms and the empirical study of social processes', in P. Hedström and R. Swedberg (eds), *Social mechanisms*. Cambridge: Cambridge University Press.

Spencer, H. 1873–1934. *Descriptive sociology*. London: various publishers.

Steel, D. P. 2008. *Across the boundaries: extrapolation in biology and the social sciences*. Oxford: Oxford University Press.

Stigler, G. J. and Becker, G. S. 1977. 'De gustibus non est disputandum', *American Economic Review* 67: 76–90.

Stigler, S. M. 1999. 'Statistical concepts in psychology', in S. M. Stigler (ed.), *Statistics on the table: the history of statistical concepts and methods*, Cambridge, MA: Harvard University Press.

Stocké, V. 2007. 'Explaining educational decision and effects of families' social class position: an empirical test of the Breen-Goldthorpe model of educational attainment', *European Sociological Review* 23: 505–19.

Stone, R. 1997. *Some British empiricists in the social sciences, 1650–1900*. Cambridge: Cambridge University Press.

Sullivan, A. 2006. 'Students as rational decision-makers: the question of beliefs and desires', *London Review of Education* 4: 271–90.

Suppes, P. 1970. *A probabilistic theory of causality*. Amsterdam: North Holland.

Susser, M. 1998. 'Does risk factor epidemiology put epidemiology at risk?', *Journal of Epidemiology and Community Health* 52: 608–11.

Thernstrom, S. 1964. *Poverty and progress: social mobility in a nineteenth century city*. Cambridge, MA: Harvard University Press.

Thompson, R. P. 2011. 'Causality, theories and medicine', in P. M. Illari, F. Russo and J. Williamson (eds), *Causality in the sciences*. Oxford: Oxford University Press.

Thornton, A., Axinn, W. G. and Xie, Y. 2007. *Marriage and cohabitation*. Chicago, IL: University of Chicago Press.

Tilly, C. 1995. 'The bourgeois gentilshommes of revolutionary theory', in N. R. Keddie (ed.), *Debating revolutions*. New York: New York University Press.

Todd, P. M., Billari, F. C. and Simão, J. 2005. 'Aggregate age-at-marriage patterns from individual mate-search heuristics', *Demography* 42: 559–74.

Tooby, J. and Cosmides, L. 1992. 'The psychological foundations of culture', in J. H. Barkow, L. Cosmides and J. Tooby (eds), *The adapted mind*. New York: Oxford University Press.

Torssander, J. and Erikson, R. 2009. 'Stratification and mortality – a comparison of education, class, status and income', *European Sociological Review* 26: 465–74.

Torssander, J. and Erikson, R. 2010. 'Marital partner and mortality: the effects of the social positions of both spouses', *International Journal of Epidemiology and Community Health* 63: 992–8.

Treiman, D. J. 1977. *Occupational prestige in comparative perspective*. New York: Academic Press.

Tumin, M. M. 1953. 'Some principles of stratification: a critical analysis', *American Sociological Review* 18: 387–94.

Turner, J. 2007. 'Is public sociology such a good idea?', in L. T. Nichols (ed.), *Public sociology: the contemporary debate*. New Brunswick, NJ: Transaction.

Tylor, E. B. 1889. 'On a method of investigating the development of institutions: applied to laws of marriage and descent', *Journal of the Royal Anthropological Institute* 18: 245–56, 261–9.

Vansina, J. 1990. *Paths in the rain forests*. Madison, WI: University of Wisconsin Press.

Vaughan, D. 1996. *The Challenger launch decision*. Chicago, IL: University of Chicago Press.

Verein für Sozialpolitik. 1912. *Verhandlungen der Generalversammlung in Nürnberg, 1911*. Leipzig: Dunker und Humblot.

Warner, W. L. and Lunt, P. S. 1941. *The social life of a modern community*. New Haven, CT: Yale University Press.

Warner, W. L. and Lunt, P. S. 1948. *The status system of a modern community*. New Haven, CT: Yale University Press.

Watts, D. J. 2014. 'Common sense and sociological explanations', *American Journal of Sociology*, 120: 313–51.

Weber, M. 1892. *Die Verhältnisse der Landarbeiter in ostelbischen Deutschland*. Leipzig: Schriften des Vereins für Sozialpolitik.

Weber, M. 1906/1949. 'A critique of Eduard Meyer's methodological views', in *The methodology of the social sciences*. Glencoe, IL: Free Press.

Weber, M. 1908. 'Zur Psychophysik der industriellen Arbeit', *Archiv für Sozialwissenschaft und Sozialpolitik* 27: 730–70.

Weber, M. 1921/1948. 'Politics as a vocation', in H. H. Gerth and C. W. Mills (eds), *From Max Weber: essays in sociology*. London: Routledge and Kegan Paul.

Weber, M. 1922/1948. 'Science as a vocation', in H. H. Gerth and C. W. Mills (eds), *From Max Weber: essays in sociology*. London: Routledge and Kegan Paul.

Weber, M. 1922/1968. *Economy and society*. Berkeley, CA: University of California Press.

Wilkinson, R. and Pickett, K. 2010. *The spirit level: why equality is better for everyone*, 2nd edn. London: Penguin.

Winch, P. 1958. *The idea of a social science and its relation to philosophy*. London: Routledge.

Wolf, E. 1982. *Europe and the people without history*. Berkeley, CA: University of California Press.

Woolgar, S. 1988. *Science: the very idea*. London: Tavistock.

Woolrych, A. 2002. *Britain in revolution 1625–1660*. Oxford: Oxford University Press.

Worrall, J. 2007. 'Evidence in medicine and evidence-based medicine', *Philosophy Compass* 6: 981–1022.

Wright, E. O. (ed.) 2005. *Approaches to class analysis*. Cambridge: Cambridge University Press.

Wright, J. D. and Marsden, P. V. 2010. 'Survey research and social science: History, current practice and future prospects', in P. V. Marsden and J. D. Wright (eds), *Handbook of survey research*. Bingley: Emerald.

Wright Mills, C. 1959. *The sociological imagination*. New York: Oxford University Press.

Wrong, D. 1961. 'The oversocialized conception of man in modern sociology', *American Sociological Review* 26: 183–93.

Wrong, D. 1999. *The oversocialized conception of man*. New Brunswick, NJ: Transaction.

Wu, L. 2000. 'Some comments on "Sequence analysis and optimal matching methods in sociology: Review and prospect"', *Sociological Methods and Research* 29: 41–64.

Xie, Y. 2000. 'Demography: past, present and future', *Journal of the American Statistical Association* 95: 670–3.

Xie, Y. 2005. 'Methodological contradictions in contemporary sociology', *Michigan Quarterly Review*, XLIV: 506–11.

Xie, Y. 2007. 'Otis Dudley Duncan's legacy: the demographic approach to quantitative reasoning in social science', *Research in Social Stratification and Mobility* 25: 141–56.

Yin, R. K. 2003. *Case study research*. Thousand Oaks, CA: Sage.

Young, M. and Willmott, P. 1957. *Family and kinship in East London*. London: Routledge.

Ziman, J. 1968. *Public knowledge: the social dimension of science*. Cambridge: Cambridge University Press.

Zonabend, F. 1992. 'The monograph in European ethnography', *Current Sociology* 40: 49–54.

Index

Soc Meth

Bias: Sampling thing
- Infinite # of samples
- any point on the solution line is unforced

Biased: In a structural model sense

- "Consistency"
- recovery the underlying structural parameters

Bryk & Raudenbush

① - Mason & Feinberg
   - Frequency vanishes
   - Setting coeff. to zero

Myth of APC Model ! Solution like
② ① solution like
   ② Perhaps beliefs no... m

② Myth of APC Model Bounds

③ Mech. & Bounds

④ IIS / RDS

⑤ IIS / RDS

⑥ Conclusion

Appendix chapters:
   A. Solution like
   B. The IVE

Cohoorts:

Pg. 13
Pg. 15 (footnote)

Pg. 82